Wakefield Press

Over 60

Joy Noble, AM, and David Bennett have both written and edited a number of books over the years. You guessed it; they are both over 60 and aiming to live life to the full.

Over 60

Living Life to the Full

Edited by
Joy Noble and David Bennett

Wakefield Press

Wakefield Press
16 Rose Street
Mile End
South Australia 5031
www.wakefieldpress.com.au

First published 2017

Text and cover designed by David Bradbury (www.dbtype.com.au)
Edited by Julia Beaven, Wakefield Press
Typeset by Michael Deves, Wakefield Press

National Library of Australia Cataloguing-in-Publication entry

Title:	Over 60: living life to the full / edited by Joy Noble and David Bennett.
ISBN:	978 1 74305 479 6 (paperback).
Subjects	Social perception in old age.
	Motivation (Psychology) in old age.
	Aging – Popular works.
	Aging – Psychological aspects.
Other Creators/ Contributors:	Bennett, David, 1941– , editor.
	Noble, Joy, 1925– , editor.

To all the writers who contributed an enormous amount of work and inspiration to make this book, and to all those over sixty seeking to live life to the full.

Contents

Foreword

This is a book about people who are doing things they didn't expect to be doing, and it's working well for them. It's also a book about those people living their lives in much the same way they always have, but now with more insight – wisdom even – leading to deeper meaning and enjoyment. Some of the contributors are making a difference to the lives of others in ways they didn't have time for earlier – because these are stories about people older than 60 years and, in some instances, 70 years. Many of them have 'retired', which means they are not doing the paid work they did for most of their life (although quite a few are being paid to do something else). This book of true stories tells of those engaged with life, who are living their lives to the full and looking forward to what they do every day. They are living lives of interest that are worth reading about.

So why conceive and edit such a book? Why have Joy Noble and David Bennett cajoled twenty-five people to write for this book; chased down stragglers (like this author); convinced the wonderful Wakefield Press to publish it; and planned, undoubtedly, to spend much time promoting it?

Well, dear potential or already committed reader, because prevailing paradigms in our society still see the people whose stories are within as being unusual or somewhat remarkable because all the contributors are 'old' – so-called. When you are old you are supposed to slow down, put your feet up, and smell the roses, because you are now 'on the slippery slope', 'over the hill', or you've entered 'God's waiting room'. The basic message is that you are past your best-by date and there's no going back.

That paradigm is changing, but it's still there and still far too prevalent, perhaps even still dominant. So Joy and David have put together a book that doesn't reek of the exceptional or miraculous but does show unequivocally that people like you and me just need to get on with life in what may be its later years, but are still years of challenge, new insights, learning, loving, joy and contribution. Indeed, as one contributor says, the first sixty years was just the warm-up for however many more are to come.

Life is for living to the full and what has age got to do with that? Nothing, other than that a learning person, which we should all be, always, will figure out how to be wiser, freer and smarter as the years proceed – and learn how to live life to the full, or indeed to the fullest, at every point.

Ian Yates, AM
Chief Executive
COTA Australia

BUSILY TAKING IT SLOWLY

JULIE FRANCIS

'Are you nearly a hundred, Babar?' my three-year-old granddaughter asked me quizzically. Here I was just turned seventy and still feeling young at heart. I smiled as I reflected on how the young see us as we age.

I still feel the same as I felt when I was a young. I remember the excited teenager thinking about fashion and boys, the bride with plans and expectations, and the new parent with hopes and dreams. Certainly back then, thinking about life after sixty was not ever on the radar.

Trying to be a good daughter, student, friend, wife, mother, homemaker, hostess, employee and so on, left little time to get off a merry-go-round of busyness – and I loved it! Being busy brings its own adrenalin rush and being busy has always been on my agenda.

Mine is a life of creativity and fulfilment; feeling useful, contributing, 'making a difference' in my world. There have been difficult times: financial struggles, living with a mortgage, renovating houses, juggling work and family, the heartbreak of divorce, and learning through it all to become strong and resilient. And in the busyness of that time in my life, the thought of being free of diaries, daily work commitments, seemed like a rainbow on the horizon ... that I would find one day.

When I celebrated reaching sixty years I was still working, my daughters had spread their wings and flown the nest, and I found a new freedom. But I still had the passion for my work, which upon reflection I realise, I have been fortunate to have always enjoyed. Moving outside my comfort zone, enjoying challenges, and sometimes going 'where angels fear to tread', as someone once said of me, is hard to cast aside.

Squashed into my working life I made sure I found time to immerse myself in my garden – the place where I restore my soul. How magical it is to get hands in the soil, plant and weed, (yes and I even enjoy weeding!), water, watch new growth, pick the blooms, and all the while watch the differences with the changing of seasons. I often marvel at the happiness and contentment I find in my back yard.

In that period my younger daughter married a Thai man in Thailand. It was a wedding of difference, exquisite and memorable, at seven in the morning in a Buddhist ceremony in a temple that jutted out on a lake, surrounded by tall trees, birds and flowers. Naturally I travelled to tourist spots, but with the benefit of Thai family members who live there, I went to places not usually frequented by travellers and experienced such a different way of life.

I just knew when I was ready to say goodbye to the paid workforce. As I farewelled my work colleagues on the eve of my sixty fifth birthday, I remember feeling liberated and exhilarated at the thought of a different life. There was an excitement about the unknown, and a sense of expectation outside the paid working world – all that I had known for some forty-five years.

What surprised me was a comment made by a colleague after I finished my farewell speech. It was from a young woman in her mid thirties, and has stayed with me: 'Thank you; your inspiring words have made me appreciate that getting old and retiring can be exciting and it's not the end'. The end?!

Since retiring my life has taken a new direction and philosophy. It's now about living in the moment and valuing the simple things. It's about going at a slower pace and having time to notice and savour the things around me. I place a different emphasis on things that I once considered so important. I don't bother about what people think of me, and feel I am free to be able to delete from my life those things that I don't want to do. There's no doubt that financial security makes a difference as to how one can spend this chapter of life, but how we think about this time is free.

The past seven years have brought me a special contentment and opened doors to new experiences. There is more time for friendships, gardening, entertainment, learning croquet, walks on the beach, some travel (especially to a music festival in Eastern Europe) and volunteering. Of course there's a list of projects that, in my working life I always planned to do, but never got around to! Funny though, somehow now with the time to do many of the things I'd planned, it's easy to say 'I can do that tomorrow'. There is a luxury in waking up most days from the sunshine beaming through my window – when I'm ready, and not when the alarm tells me it's time to rise.

I love my daily trips to local cafés for a morning coffee, reading the papers, doing crosswords and keeping up with the latest in AFL football. How exciting are the winter months following my Crows. My friends laugh at me adapting my social life around the AFL calendar. I've loyally attended matches at West Lakes for years, but now I delight in the amazing experience at the Adelaide Oval. Walking across the bridge with thousands, surrounded by colour and buzz and hearing the noise, oh the noise, takes me to another world for a few hours. Usually the next week I enjoy a post mortem, comparing footy tips at the local café with new-found friends. With the luxury of some great cafés within walking distance from

A restoration of love

home, I now have time to drink good coffee and listen to the young (well, they always seem so young!) skilled coffee makers talking about their lives and dreams. It's so interesting hearing the views of younger people. In my other life I would have paid for a coffee with a polite thank you and been off in a hurry.

I restored my daughters' dolls' house, one that forty years ago we had found at a rubbish dump and had provided years of fun, but which had sat long neglected in the shed. I discovered a dolls' house industry and was fascinated with the women I met who have made it a lifetime hobby. My project was merely to restore and decorate this eighty-year-old, two-storey house made from old timber floorboards so my grandchildren could play.

I have time for visits to the library for new computer courses and to improve skills in my long held interest in photography. My obsession with jigsaws, at times intense, can be sporadic. And as for technology, I remember when as a young teenager my parents installed our first telephone. It was a black Bakelite and placed on a special table in the hallway and oh how excited we were when it first rang! I thought we were so rich! Of course manners required taking a message at mealtimes and being aware that confidential conversations could be easily overheard by other family members. How different is our world today!

After years of responsibility throughout my life, in my retirement I have opted to let others do the leading. Feeling useful and making a contribution has found me working in the local school tuckshop, being in the box office at a local cinema and making 'jumbo choc tops' in the candy bar. More recently it's as a volunteer compere in a community radio station, where over sixties provide easy listening music and information to over sixties. Challenging and what fun!

Expectations have changed, patience has improved, but tolerance is probably going downhill! I essentially feel the same person as when I was young, but there is a mellowness and wisdom that I find refreshing.

Love and activity, in whatever form they take, are to me such important ingredients in living life to the full. I've talked about activity, but I have been blessed with love. Love of parents now since gone, love of friends both male and female, but especially love of my daughters and three granddaughters. To be involved in their lives, listening to their ups and downs, sharing in their achievements, their joys and disappointments, gives me more than money can buy.

A caring and loving family was a high priority passed on to me from my family. So babysitting for me is more than merely minding grandchildren. It is floating paper boats in the gutter on a rainy day, listening to squeals of delight as we collect sea shells to make necklaces, taking them to the theatre, together making our first cumquat marmalade, playing dress-ups, and acting out fairy stories and reading books to them (and now listening to them read to me). I have been known to answer the door with fairy wings and a tiara, gone to the park with teddy bears piled in an old wicker pram for a 'teddy bears' picnic'. I've loved attending Grandparents' Day at the school, picking up after school for ballet lessons, making 'jelly oranges' for birthday parties, cooking with little ones and not being fussed with flour and cocoa all over the floor, and together decorating my house and tree at Christmas time – and oh so much more! To give them a sense of their history, a sense of belonging is important to me, but to listen and learn from my adult daughters and granddaughters is inspiring.

Yes I'm over sixty, and yes, I'm living life to the full!

TRAVEL AND TECHNOLOGY ARE GOOD FOR OUR BRAINS IN THE LAST THIRD OF OUR LIVES

JONATHAN ANDERSON

I have been lucky in my job and during my childhood to have travelled extensively, but on entering the third stage of my life – as many others discover – travel has taken on an even more prominent role. Travel broadens the mind, opens new horizons, stimulates you, and offers fresh experiences. Journeys abroad increase your knowledge of other cultures, traditions and customs, as well as giving opportunities to learn about the history and geography of other lands and to practise language skills.

Arthur Frommer, author of the original *Europe on 5 Dollars A Day* (an amount that has sharply increased over the years), adds that through travel we learn that all people in the world are basically alike, but that not everyone shares our beliefs. Travel Editor for the *Weekend Australian*, Susan Kurosawa, puts it differently. Travel, she says, helps us to celebrate differentness and it tests our level of tolerance and self-awareness. By giving you greater understanding, travel expands your brain.

While still working full-time as Professor at Flinders University I put forward a suggestion to WEA, an adult learning and educational centre in South Australia, for a tour to South America. This idea grew out of a long-held interest in the Incas dating from early childhood. I called the tour *In the Footsteps of the Incas*. The core of the itinerary I suggested was to start at Sun Island in Lake Titicaca in Bolivia where according to legend the Incas originated, circle Lake Titicaca to the Peruvian side following in the footsteps of the first Inca, Manco Capac and his sister/wife Mama Ocllo, continue to Cuzco where they founded what became the Inca empire, and conclude with the pinnacle of Inca achievement at Machu Picchu. To my surprise, the suggestion was soon taken up and I was asked to lead the tour. So began a more than twenty-year-long association with WEA Travel.

In retirement without the constraints of going to work each day, opportunities to travel to different corners of the globe multiplied. For WEA, I have now led seven tours following *In the Footsteps of the Incas*, and a total of thirty international tours. However, it's not the amount of travel that is critical but the ways travel helps keep one's brain active and invigorated. Travel has brought for me many memorable moments. One was an unusual and rather special graduation ceremony in Africa.

No one on the first tour I led for WEA to Namibia expected to attend a graduation ceremony since the tour was billed as an adventure safari. However, three months before leaving on tour, one of my post-graduate students, Petrina, the first student to attend Flinders University from Namibia, received reports from two external examiners passing her Master's thesis. Knowing that Petrina would be unable to return to Adelaide for her graduation, the Vice-Chancellor agreed for me to arrange an informal ceremony for her in Windhoek, and suggested I take the university banner and a mortar board and academic gown for Petrina. Tour members had met Petrina at a pre-tour meeting and when they heard of the award to be conferred all opted to come to the informal graduation ceremony that was planned. Petrina's family put on a typical bush meal and decorated the hall around the Flinders banner.

Graduation ceremony in Windhoek, Namibia, while on safari: Petrina receives a bound copy of her thesis

Surrounded by friends and family plus the WEA group, Petrina received her degree, not the official parchment, but a bound copy of her thesis. For all tour members, the evening provided a fun introduction to local people, customs and food, with a touch of colour for never before has a tour leader gone on safari with full academic robes and regalia.

A WEA tour to Cuba provided memorable moments of a different kind. One of the hotels we stayed at was the historic Sevilla in the old quarter of Havana. The hotel was celebrating its hundredth year and many were the stories its walls could tell, for in the swinging years before the revolution that swept Castro into power it was the

Lifted aloft on tour of Thailand's Golden Triangle.

favourite of the rich and famous. One couple in our group stayed in Room 501, secret meeting place in Graham Greene's *Our Man in Havana*. My wife and I had Room 601, which had been Al Capone's suite when he and his bodyguards occupied the whole of the sixth floor at the end of the twenties. Staying at the Sevilla Hotel was like being part of history. Strolling from the hotel down graceful Prado Avenue brings one to Gran Teatro, one of the world's grand opera houses. What better way to see inside this great theatre than go to a performance and be part of an enthusiastic, highly passionate, Cuban audience. All these were magical moments.

A real delight when travelling is to do or experience something that is completely out of the ordinary. A stand-out, adrenalin-filled, fun activity for me happened on a tour to the Golden Triangle region in northern Thailand when I went on an elephant safari. I had ridden elephants before but this time I rode bareback for the first time. We learned how to mount an elephant, putting one foot on its knee and, as it raised its leg upwards, throwing the other foot over the elephant's back while firmly clutching its ears. With one rider per elephant, I tucked my knees behind the elephant's ears and held on firmly to the elephant's round head. We headed off into the jungle through dense undergrowth and up into the hills, a mahout walking alongside. It was an experience like no other! But the best was still to come because on the return journey we traversed a river and now it was time to wash our elephants. While in the river, we mounted the elephant in a different way, climbing onto its trunk and then lifted high above the elephant's head. It was a heart-in-the-mouth, fun-filled moment.

In a similar way that travel expands your brain, technology likewise is good brain food. One of my students once told me in the early days of computers in schools that the computer is our second brain. Why then don't we all embrace information and communication technologies wholeheartedly? Actually, young people do. They are digital natives having grown up with the new technologies all around them. But for digital immigrants like many of my generation, there is often a fear about the new and unfamiliar. It has always been so. The philosopher Socrates warned against the newfangled invention of writing, telling his students that it would impair their memory. I have a treasured book on my bookshelves in which my great-grandfather urges parents in the Shetland Islands to continue telling their bairns, round the blazing peat fire, tales of trows and witches and spirits, warning them that the young folk no longer listen: they read. In a similar vein, I remember as a boy on a visit to the Shetlands my grandpa warning me about ballpoint pens that had begun to appear. 'Don't ever use them in exams,' he said, 'because they can run out, not like pen and ink.'

New electronic devices like tablets and smart phones – all information and communication tools – shape the way our brains receive information and work with information. Consider how the invention of writing made us less reliant on memory; how the introduction of the printing press made stores of knowledge accessible to all of us; how the invention of the telegraph carried information to us rapidly over vast distances; and how television brought information right into the home. Now, computers and the internet bring information directly to our fingertips. All these information tools change the way our brain receives and handles information. They open new pathways in our brains.

My favourite travel companion these days, after my wife of course, is my iPhone. Connect to wireless networks – now available almost everywhere – in most hotels and libraries, in many restaurants, cafés, public buildings and shopping centres, on some buses, trains and ferries, even in certain public parks – and you have a super smart travelling companion ready to serve you. In recent travels, I have used my iPhone:

- as an atlas, street directory, and direction finder
- to take notes and write a daily diary
- to send and receive emails
- for dictating emails and notes
- to chat with family and friends using Skype or FaceTime
- as a timepiece, alarm clock, even a stopwatch
- to read daily news reports and updates
- to play music
- to see video clips or even full-length movies

- to check the time anywhere in the world from Albania to Zimbabwe
- as a calculator
- to make currency conversions
- to translate foreign words and phrases
- as an encyclopedia, dictionary or thesaurus
- as a library resource to read books I have stored on the device
- as a weather barometer
- as a camera
- to store photographs and display pictures in a slideshow.

All of this in a device that fits in your pocket! Further, your smart phone can perform all these tasks at no cost everywhere that public internet is available. And, incidentally, smart phones can be used to make telephone calls too, but these use phone networks and do incur a cost.

If we could wind back the clock two decades, the world had no worldwide web, internet or email. A decade ago, there were no smart phones, electronic books were a rarity, and social media like FaceBook and Twitter were yet to be invented. Imagine what new technologies and applications might emerge in the decades ahead. It is an exciting prospect. Travel, together with these new technologies, help keep one young and in touch with the younger generation.

SINGING IN THE SYDNEY OPERA HOUSE

ANNETTE DAY

Singing has always been a part of my life. I can remember my mum and dad singing, whistling (Dad), or humming around the house. Mum played the piano and my sister, brother and I enjoyed singing the nursery rhymes and other songs we were taught. Dad loved serenading Mum with 'If you were the only girl in the world and I were the only boy'. We three children would giggle.

Grandma and Grandpa were also musical and they had a pianola. Grandpa used to play his fiddle whilst pumping the pianola pedals with his feet and we'd sing along to the rolls.

Of course there was plenty of singing at our local Methodist Church with rousing hymns, catchy choruses and huge Sunday School anniversaries. I used to sing in the church choir and was fortunate enough to sing in my primary school choir that performed in two consecutive years at the Adelaide Town Hall Combined Schools Concerts. At my high school we had a very competent music teacher who composed operas and I had great fun singing in the chorus of three of them.

In my late teens I took singing lessons for a time and joined a big Adelaide choir but then work took me to the country where I was involved with smaller choirs. When my children came along I went back to singing around the house. At fifty I joined another

Practising for ChorusOz

big Adelaide choir. It is fun being with like-minded people who love to sing and learning new pieces is so good for concentration. There's no time to think of world problems, and I come home from rehearsals feeling refreshed. Being in the choir has given me the opportunity to perform with them at many wonderful venues around Adelaide, South Australian country towns and even interstate.

Over the years the choir has invited choirs from the USA, Holland and Japan to perform with us and I've happily hosted choristers from these countries. In return I was able to holiday with my new friends in Holland and Japan. We didn't have much English between us but I still attended their choir practices and joined in when it was in Latin or German. My hosted friends have remained friends to this day.

I'm still singing in my choir but last year at seventy I took a happy diversion and signed up to sing with 'ChorusOz' at the Sydney Opera House Concert Hall over the June long weekend. In total there were six hundred choristers from all around Australia with about a dozen from overseas. The planning for this big event was amazing. To be included you had to be able to hold a tune and love singing.

The printed music for the Rutter 'Gloria' and Duruflé 'Requiem' duly arrived with my soprano part on a CD that I could sing along with. Fortunately I already knew the 'Gloria' but hadn't even heard the 'Requiem' before so I was eager to get started. Sometimes I practised with my sister and other people who were involved. Then it was time to go.

ChorusOz at Sydney Opera House. Photo George Gonczi

The Saturday morning was for enrolling and collecting our special T-shirts and the afternoon was down to work. The sopranos practised at a school auditorium where there were two grand pianos on stage and we sat or stood in the auditorium enjoying the directions of our wonderful conductor, Brett Weymark.

We had to be at the Opera House bright and early Sunday morning to be correctly seated, and then the whole choir sang with two grand pianos. It sounded wonderful. It was even more exciting when the talented soloists joined us. After morning tea we were accompanied by the Sydney Philharmonia Orchestra and organ. That rehearsal didn't go as well, but after lunch we improved markedly. We had a quick afternoon tea before the performance at five pm.

The crescendo the choristers gave the first 'Gloria' nearly took the roof off and I felt tingling up and down my spine. Our charismatic conductor was beaming as we followed him faithfully to the tumultuous applause at the end. Again Brett conducted us brilliantly through the divine 'Requiem' music. It was exhilarating to sing in the world famous Opera House and I shared the experience with my beloved younger sister by my side.

Next year our choir has been invited to sing with the Japanese choir that we know. I'm looking forward to singing with them again and catching up with my Japanese friends.

PAST, PRESENT, FUTURE

GAVIN SCRIMGEOUR

After forty-three years as a secondary teacher, I was still enjoying being in the classroom – but well and truly over the marking, preparation, meetings and all the minutiae which go with being in a school. When I found that I was no longer looking forward to the possibilities of new classes at the beginning of a new school year, I knew the time was right to finish. So I entered retirement with many memories and a feeling of satisfaction about my teaching career, but with no regrets about leaving it behind.

I was looking forward to whatever came next, but although I had some broad ideas, I had no specific plans. The inevitable well-intentioned and often asked question, 'What are you going to do?' (and later, 'What do you do with your time?') became an annoyance. It seemed that there was the expectation that I should have the next few years mapped out, a list of goals that I was working towards and activities to work through, and even an implication that if I didn't, I was in danger of succumbing to boredom and vegetating towards an early death! I answered in the usual generalities (travel, fixing things around the house, doing some writing, catching up on reading, reading the paper (online) properly, doing some relief teaching – no, I don't play golf). This may have satisfied my questioners, but it irked me because I felt I was unnecessarily being put on the spot.

A mapped-out program was not how I saw the future – I had had forty-three years of that! What lay ahead was much less specific – a freedom to pursue my own interests, to do what I wanted to do, to take advantage of opportunities as they arose, without pressure, at my own pace, without time constraints and with fewer boundaries. And the options now are so many, and so easily accessed, that there has never been one day when I have felt at a loose end. Yes, there have been the occasional days when I have not done much – but that has been my choice.

Some of my time has been spent on fairly solitary interests. I have done a lot of writing. One of my loves is history, and although I like to have some understanding of events, my main interest is not in political, military or economic machinations. Rather it is in the often extraordinary experiences of ordinary people caught up in events of their own or others making.

One thing I wish I had done while I was teaching was to record the many stories of danger, courage and survival I was told by refugee students. The Vietnamese girl whose father jumped overboard from their boat as her mother and older sister were raped by Thai pirates; the Cambodian family who, as they escaped across a minefield, took turns in the lead as they followed exactly the footsteps of the person in front of them; the El Salvadorean girl who saw her teacher dragged off the bus on the way to school and who was never seen again; the Iraqi father with a very traumatised young son bursting into tears as he grasped and stared through a high wire fence which reminded him of horrendous months at Port Hedland Detention Centre; the young Sudanese woman who, when a very young girl, was permanently separated from her family when a large refugee group was attacked from the air while camped in a river bed in Ethiopia. These were stories that should not be forgotten, stories about real people, not the depersonalised and demonised 'illegal arrivals' we are encouraged to reject. It is now too late for me to record them, but this has encouraged me to try to document parts of my own family history.

I have tracked my maternal grandfather's experiences in the AIF in the First World War. None of his letters from the time have survived and he never talked about his experiences on the Western Front, and I certainly never thought to ask him. He died when I was nineteen, during the 1960s, the time of Vietnam, conscription and moratorium marches. In our anti-war sentiment ANZAC Day was seen by my generation as an excuse for old men to go out and get drunk, and we rarely thought about the sacrifices made and the traumas endured by those who had done what they believed was their duty and put their lives on hold to enlist. All we knew of Gramp's war was that he had been wounded in the buttock – and of course we joked he was 'running away'.

But he did leave a tiny 1917 diary. This diary has only very occasional brief entries about daily events, but, remarkably, it also contains a meticulous record of his movements during the three-and-a-half years he was overseas. This list of 186 dates and locations means we know where he was for every night of the time he was away. With the help of digitised Army records now available online, the surviving letters and reminiscences of other members of his battalion and the ever-increasing number of secondary sources, I have been able to write a detailed account of what his war may have been like. There is much satisfaction in paying this tribute to him and knowing that his experiences and sacrifices will now be remembered.

The research was amazingly satisfying, full of discovery and surprises. A photograph taken in Egypt of his section (the only photo I found of any section in his battalion) was an exciting find, but trumped by the time I realised that maps I was looking at in the digitised 8th Brigade diary had been drawn by my grandfather while on detachment as a draughtsman to Brigade Headquarters. I got some guilty pleasure by working out what he was up to when he went AWL while on leave in England and conjecturing about his romantic attachments.

Most importantly, Gramp was with the 32nd Battalion from its formation. Immediately after its arrival on the Western Front the battalion lost ninety per cent of its fighting strength at the pointless (and for many years almost forgotten) Battle of Fromelles, the deadliest twenty-four hours in Australian military history. It is probable that Gramp was 'lucky' to be wounded by heavy shelling in the trenches before he reached the frontline, and did not go 'over the top'. Despite this, I am sure that the Battle was the most significant event of the war for him and understanding of his experience required a knowledge of the men of the 32nd and of Fromelles. This became an important 'flow-on' interest to me, and also something I hope I can explore further in the future.

My latest family history project, with my wife Lian, is to record what we can about her family in Indonesia. She grew up in difficult circumstances in West Java, and it is important that her memories, and the memories and stories of her ancestors from a different culture and time, be recorded for her descendants.

One of the biggest differences for the current generation of older Australians compared to previous generations is the possibility and ease of travel, often with the added incentive of visiting children living and working overseas. So it is not surprising that Lian and I spend two or three months every year travelling overseas, including visiting our son in Norway. Some of the fun of travel for us is the time spent beforehand planning our trip, working out an itinerary, and improving our knowledge of the countries we are going to visit. We are not traditional backpackers any more, but we do travel lightly and independently, without rushing, rarely staying in hotels, using public transport and making sure we are not confined to the main tourist destinations. There may come a time when a tour group or a cruise may be an appropriate mode of travel – but not yet. Travel for us is most satisfying when there are surprises, when there are some challenges and when we make our own decisions. It should be an adventure.

High-altitude adventurers

All of our travel has been together, apart from one trip in 2013 when Lian travelled with a friend in Turkey while my three brothers and I travelled, again independently, to Central Asia, through the fabled cities of Khiva, Bukhara and Samarkand in Uzbekistan, into Tajikistan and, following the footsteps of Marco Polo and Sven Hardin, along the border with Afghanistan into the Wakhan Valley, dotted with forts and occasional villages, and boxed in by the towering Hindu Kush. We crossed the immense, remote and incredibly scenic high altitude plateau of the Pamir Mountains, one of the highest inhabited places on earth, sleeping in local homestays, and eventually arrived in Osh in Kyrgyzstan. It was a true adventure.

I have also been lucky in that I have been able to maintain some professional responsibilities (and fund our travel) by continuing to do some work, periodically through the year but especially at exam time, for the South Australian Certificate of Education. The opportunity to continue to use my professional experience and knowledge, and to feel valued for what I do, has been important to me. I do not think it has been an essential factor in making a successful transition to retirement, but the fact that I still feel connected with what I did in my working life may have helped the transition.

Much to my surprise, I have possibly read less than before my retirement. Many of those things around the house remain to be done. Family history still fascinates me, the sorely ignored men of the 32nd Battalion deserve to have their story told, there are many more travel destinations than we will ever have time to visit. Working in the garden is rewarding relaxation – and if I want to visit someone or go out for a coffee I can. Eventually we expect our children will get around to presenting us with grandchildren! I know that, inevitably, there are going to be some more difficult and sadder times ahead, but in the meantime we have so much to look forward to in the future.

LIVING CHANGE

HELEN DISNEY

I write this as I start the last year of my sixties, wondering about my seventies. As I headed towards my sixties I had decided that it was time to do some more of the things I had been wanting to do. At that time I had been working hard in the social policy consulting company that my partner and I had started seven years earlier in Canberra. I had always wanted to work overseas but it was not until this time in my life that with the support of my partner I was able to take a radical new step and take up a short-term contract to work in Afghanistan with Save the Children UK.

So my seventh decade started as I marked my sixtieth birthday in India travelling on my own around Kerala state for a week in March 2006. I was in Kerala as a reflective break on the way home coming 'out' of Afghanistan where I had worked for three months.

I felt privileged to be in Afghanistan. It was a precious time, despite being away from family and friends, and despite and because of being aware that the whole situation in Afghanistan was so very damaging for most other people there and that numbers of people were losing their lives. Afghanistan had been living through one of the most significant and destructive developments since WWII. This was four years after the war in Afghanistan that followed 9/11 but also after twenty years of harrowing war and upheaval for Afghanistan.

One of my great interests is in social history and I was gaining firsthand, profound new understanding of the everyday effects of world changing events. The three months had been so full of intense insights into the world, people, history, geography, international politics, and life, and I was learning more about many significant things: my own and other cultures, high security settings, being in the midst of a shattered post-conflict society, living in a hard winter in very simple but surprisingly comfortable circumstances, friendship, and managing long distance relationships and communication – all at the same time.

It was an intense insight being in a society but not having access to reliable information about the major daily events there other than through those people I was working with. In the house in the suburbs of Kabul where Save the Children UK was located for security reasons, we had some international TV but I had no language to access local news that might be available. I remember thinking about how many momentous destructive events in history had been the result of rumours sweeping through communities in the absence of more information through communication channels we have relied on for more than a century – radio, newspapers and TV. And I was seeing, and talking with my Afghani colleagues about, the hard decisions they had to make about such things as staying or leaving, being out and about in their own city, risking whether to campaign as a woman for the elections in that society, trying to work to save further loss of the developed civilisation of Afghanistan.

After I returned to Australia I was asked to talk to some groups and to my dismay I didn't do justice to Afghanistan or what I had learnt. I had known that I should write about it at the time but I didn't do it and as a result I didn't record so much of my thinking and reactions so when the time came to share these I felt overwhelmed and lost in a myriad of details and memories. I wrote emails and was so glad to have the Internet to do so but I don't still have those readily accessible. I have many great digital photos and of course like many people probably I need to cull and organise these. Perhaps I will make a goal for my seventies to organise my photos and do some thinking and writing because within eighteen months of returning to Australia I went to live and work in Papua New Guinea for seven years and I have so much to process and retrieve for myself from that experience too.

Back in Australia my life was moving on very fast again as I reconnected with family and friends and was swept up again into the busy work of the consulting company. From 2006 to mid 2007 the consulting work was fast paced, varied and challenging too as we reviewed and evaluated a wide range of major programs and activities including particularly, for example, for Indigenous people and communities, young people leaving care, and people experiencing homelessness and/or mental illness. We had been doing this work for eight excitement-packed years and now we were both feeling that we wanted to move on from the demands of running our own company. We were also both interested to work in international development and we were pleased to win jobs in Papua New Guinea.

And so for my next work experiences – seven years in a society struggling to make its way forward into the world of the 21st century from its centuries-old world of hundreds of self-sufficient small rural communities. Eighty-five per cent of the population still live in rural and remote villages and are not yet part of a market economy. During my time in Port Moresby I saw the early development of a middle class with the sudden influx of cars onto the road, new shops with furniture and household goods which Papua New Guineans were buying not expatriates, the phenomenal spread of mobile phones particularly because of Digicel's entry into the market, and the increase in range of items available in supermarkets where increasing numbers of Papua New Guineans were shopping. There was also a new generation of which a larger percentage had tertiary education and, for an increasing number, education overseas to tertiary level.

PNG head-dress

I was working in the law and justice sector as part of an Australian-funded program, which at that time was combining work to build stronger institutions for law and justice in the public service in PNG, with projects and activities to build infrastructure and change service delivery approaches. I also had nearly a year in Bougainville learning more to add to the Afghanistan experience, about how challenging and arduous is the long-haul work of post-conflict recovery.

I feel very privileged to have had these two experiences in my work – experiences which were about mutual learning between myself and my 'counterparts', in Afghanistan and PNG. From Afghanistan I learnt at firsthand of the tragedy of destruction and the enormous struggle to rebuild while still riven by division. And from PNG I feel I understand better the importance of knowing about the long slow process of development in western countries in order not to load PNG with unrealistic expectations of the pace of change; and the turmoil particularly for the educated people who are trying to work out what they want for their country from overseas ideas and what they want to retain from PNG's literally very colourful and dynamic heritage – or should I say heritages with over 800 different language groups across the mainland and the islands. Some people may have read of this world for the generation exposed to colonial influence in Drusilla Modjeska's book about PNG, *The Mountain.*

I should also mention here the issue of security. In Afghanistan, life was confined and so I did not see a lot of the country although I was driven to Mazar-i-Sharif through the Hindu Kush in the snow – a stunningly beautiful world but with war ruins. And what I saw of Kabul was fascinating but heartbreaking as epitomised for me in the ruins of the palace and of the Russian-style apartment blocks. On the other hand in PNG I was able to see quite a lot of what is a very beautiful country and to live a full life in Port Moresby. We didn't walk around but we did drive and we were able to keep fit by swimming in good pools, we went sailing and snorkelling, and I took up scuba diving which is such a spectacular thing to do in the clear waters of PNG.

Throughout these years my children have been progressing in

their lives and living in other places – Australia and America – so more long distance communication and relationships. Along with other baby boomer grandparents with families spread around the world I love my Skype. My parents migrated to Australia in the fifties and had no way of keeping in touch with their parents other than letters which took weeks and phone calls that were so expensive they were only made once a year – the riotously inadequate Christmas call.

I have also been able to continue to travel – I was fortunate to travel quite a lot at various points in my life. From PNG I could have fairly regular delightful visits to see my son and his family and my friends in Canberra; and less frequent but equally delightful visits to my daughter and her family in New York and then San Diego. And then last year after finishing full time in PNG I spent a treasured two months with my daughter and her family in their new home in Nashville. I'm not sure I will have such a long time with them again – but I guess you never know. Following the time in the USA my partner and I had two great months travelling through the UK, where I was born, and across Europe to Istanbul.

I have also been part of a complex, modern, extended, blended family with stepchildren and step-grandchildren. And I have always had cousins on the other side of the world. Never a dull moment.

Now, in addition to continuing to work in PNG as a consultant on a visiting rather than in-country basis, my partner and I are establishing a base for ourselves in South Australia where I grew up. Renewing friendships and making new ones. This will perhaps be the base for the next decade of a 'full life', but I guess increasingly tempered by the ageing process.

A MARATHON LIFE

IAN NOBLE

It was while waiting for the bus on the Stresemannstrasse in Berlin, on the morning following the 2013 Berlin Marathon, that the reality of my running journey suddenly dawned on me.

Perhaps it was the young well-dressed couple from Brazil sitting opposite to me. They were on the same marathon package tour as myself, and were independently absorbed on their mobile devices, seated next to a faded and almost disused yellow Berlin postbox. They had no understanding that this postbox once had a glorious and significant past as the starting point for travellers to communicate their exploits to family and friends via handwritten and individually addressed postcards. These postcards would have depicted chocolate box scenes of a romantic Berlin, which often arrived many weeks later, if at all. In sharp contrast the communications this couple was sending instantly to all their friends were electronic versions of hundreds of postcards, displaying their personal images of Berlin, borne from the seemingly endless number of photos they had recorded on their smartphone.

Or perhaps my awakening was due to the aura of their very new, brightly colored matching designer suitcases, that looked like all one had to do was program in the next destination and the suitcase would meet you there. These suitcases, which I knew from conversations with the couple, contained their nutrients, shoes, running tops, Ultra Violet protection sunglasses, compression running stockings, gloves, arm and leg warmers, souvenir jackets, all suitably fashionably matched by colour, style and brand. As well as the nutrients and attire the suitcase inevitably included personal attachable running computers and other devices or applications that monitored all aspects of their running performance, history and personal best achievements.

By comparison my well-travelled and worn suitcase of some twenty years still required my focused efforts to get it onto the bus and then on to the next destination. It contained the same running shorts I always used, one pair of shoes, gloves, a hat, and some old warm top to dispose off at the start of the race. I considered a performance device too difficult to program or even read without fumbling around for my spectacles, and special nutrients, all too hard. I preferred to stay with my usual dietary habits.

It was at this juncture in my thoughts that I realised that in the world of running I had become, like my old suitcase, just luggage.

Like my suitcase I had travelled to marathons, half marathons, and runs in Australia, mostly Melbourne, but also across the world, observing and being entwined in the social and technological changes engulfing our running world, but never having a say or input in the progress of change. Whereas running was once a lone and individual sport, and marathons in particular were considered the ultimate running test seemingly run by fanatics, the marathon was now a spectacle, a show, a festival, a calendar event.

From New York to Boston, to Tokyo, Berlin, Chicago and London, to name the linked six major marathons, each festival starts with the hall of exhibits where you retrieve your race pack, then meander through colourful and noisy retail stalls. The young participants – and there are so many of them – take the opportunity to purchase all kinds of wondrous articles to enhance their dress, diet, training, preparation, and final performance. Each three or four day festival moves through friendship runs, numerous pre race pasta dinners, tours of the track, the march of nations, lectures on performance, appearances by the odd old marathon star, and so on, until finally we get to race day. As luggage, I just pass through or ignore these activities like a suitcase moving timelessly around and around on a carousel.

In the larger international marathons, race day usually starts with a 5:30 am breakfast, before we wait in long lines to board the buses to the starting areas, a scene of tents, toilets, festivity and of course hundreds of volunteers decked out in their bright marathon uniforms. In Tokyo in 2014, the number of volunteers seemed to far outweigh the 35,000 competitors. These enthusiastic and always invariably young volunteers direct, feed, water, manage your clothing, as well as assist in providing all level of support in photographing, timing, analysing and communicating to you, your run performance. From the starting areas, we are then herded to the corrals for a further long and cold wait, to be released in waves, the elite runners having already long departed.

But each race is individual. In New York, the 2011 marathon attracted a crowd of two million people as it wound its way through the five boroughs. It is a wonderful feeling running with an enthusiastic crowd, accompanied by one hundred and thirty bands over the course, before the final run through Central Park to the finish.

Boston in particular is significant. This is the runners' race, where usually one needs to qualify to be selected for the race, being the most prestigious marathon in the world. In 2013, I had finished the run, and was changing in the Lennox Hotel that fronts the finishing line when the two bombs went off. I was evacuated from the hotel, and spent the next nine hours in a world of panic and confusion as the authorities strove to control and resolve the crisis. Never had such an event been shaken by such a violent incident.

In Harlem

Perhaps I need to concentrate on races like the Havana Half Marathon, which I ran in 2011. Here the race remains for the moment in the past, where the participants, whilst poorly dressed, are enthusiastic and friendly. We run over a seemingly random course that just weaves its way through the chaotic traffic, where one has to watch out for potholes, lest you fall in and disappear from the face of the planet, and where one can expect the unexpected. As for a hall of exhibits, fashion and running paraphilia, race tracking and even toilets; no chance, at least you won't be luggage there.

Each race brings me alive. For this time I'm not luggage. It is here that I breathe in the air of a new city, hear the crowd, feel the pounding of my feet, and sense the pain and tiredness coming around the 36 km mark. At this point the race demands mental as well as physical strength. I draw on all my resources to reach that 42.2 km finish line. An encouraging and supportive crowd spurs me on to a sprint to the end as I try to achieve another personal best. Crossing the line, the photos are snapped, the official time recorded, the sample bag handed out. The race is finished for me now, and the exiting processes take over, the carousel whirrs back into action, and once again I become luggage.

I will continue to run for as long as I can, for as long as the legs, or the money, and the spirit will allow ... I may even have to buy myself a new suitcase.

CRUISING, GUIDING, DANCING – ON MY TERMS

PAT SMYTH

On the first Monday of the week after I retired I lay back in my bed and relaxed completely. After years of getting up at 6 am and catching the 7.30 am bus in all sorts of weather, did I enjoy that extra time in bed! However I still wake up at 5 am.

No more telephones or worrying about other people's appointments.

The week after I retired I met a lady at a daytime yoga class who volunteered in a museum, and she said they were looking for volunteers. I filled in the necessary paperwork, got my police clearance and fourteen years later I am still volunteering. I am fortunate in that I use a computer and have actually updated my experience through the various assignments that have come my way at the museum. The people I work with are very supportive and great fun.

I have been on many holidays since retiring, both within Australia and overseas. London is always my favourite destination as I know my way around quite well. A highlight of a recent cruise was a stopover at St Petersburg and a visit to the Hermitage Museum. A magnificent place; one could spend a week there and only touch the surface. All the rooms were guarded by grim-looking Russian attendants who took their roles very seriously.

Volunteering at Subiaco Museum

I enjoy line dancing which I started before I retired. Now I go to several classes a week and this keeps me pretty fit. I have made quite a few friends and attend socials and balls several times during the year. I know some ladies who just live for dancing.

About seven years ago I went on a cruise to Vanuatu and other islands with a large group of line dancers.

I went to Bolton, near Manchester, in 2011 with several members from one of the clubs I attend for a week of social dancing and competition. This was most enjoyable (despite the fact I was not feeling too well) and it was good to meet the local line dancing groups. To go from one side of the world to the other and do the same dances shows how small the world is. At times we had trouble with the accent but we managed quite well.

Bolton has a very interesting museum. This features the city during the time when the main industry was the cotton mills. Times must have been so hard. Of particular interest was the age of the children; they were working in the mills from about the age of six years.

Tamworth in New South Wales has a festival in January centred around country and western music and line dancing and I have been there three times. I love the country and the feeling of space and the leisurely pace. The town is buzzing with life and music for about ten days and the buses run all night with people attending the concerts and sporting clubs.

I have met a lot of retired people through my exercise classes and my volunteer work and never cease to be amazed about how knowledgeable and enthusiastic they are. Often one of the ladies will disappear from the class for a couple of weeks. They have done one of two things: been on holiday or had a hospital stay. There is never any complaining about aches and pains – they just get on with it. We have a very enthusiastic gym teacher who has us lifting weights, juggling, playing tunnel ball, dancing etc.

I have had time to look after my garden, although raking up leaves and pruning seem to be the major tasks. So far I have resisted buying a computer because I can go to the library but will have to bite the bullet and go online. I am now reading more and must have my daily newspaper to work on puzzles and crosswords. I am quite a coffee/food expert as I can now have a cup of coffee or lunch with friends and not have to worry about rushing back to the office.

One of the downsides is the loss of several of my friends. This brings home the fact that we are not immortal and should enjoy life while we can.

However, the best thing about life after work is the freedom I have to spend with my family and friends.

SIXTY AND OTHER RUDE WORDS

LYNN SMAILES

Hi Paul

Thanks for another email reminder about your sixtieth. Is this viral marketing? Man, we dig. Not only that, it is fab, groovy, peachy keen, far out, grouse, rad, awesome and cool. We have pencilled your party into our diary, which is overcrowded with Centrelink reporting dates, medical appointments and lunches rather than dinners. We are looking forward to going out at night, but a little bit scared. Not really. In fact, if I ever say that to you, to use my mother's words, 'Please shoot me.'

Sweet sixty. I know why I hadn't noticed it approaching – I'm still thirty in my head. There are signs others don't see me the way I see myself, including reports in the news media referring to 'elderly' people of sixty doing this or that. I'm with Patricia Edgar, ambassador for The National Ageing Research Institute and author of *In Praise of Ageing*, when she declares at fifty 'we are entering the second half of life, not heading for the scrap heap' and 'the term old should perhaps mean someone over eighty-five, not sixty-five and certainly not fifty-five'. I doubt my eighty-five-year-old friend would agree with this – he only stopped working as an anaesthetist last year.

Changes in spoken and written language are another reminder of my change in status. Younger people have always developed their own dialect to bypass or protect their elders – in recent times the dialect has included acronyms designed to extract maximum value from text messages, Facebook posts and Tweets. At some point I made the transition to being one of the protected ones and was baffled by what WTF and NFI stood for, although, in terms of LOL, I still favour 'lots of love' ahead of 'laughing out loud'. In a sign I have crossed the line to become an opinionated older person, I regard insult by acronym as a poor substitute for fully spelt out words that were once deemed rude or obscene. Despite the fact that some younger people use these words so casually in conversation, they are startled when I spit them out with such satisfaction. This is invariably when something – usually a computerised 'thingo' – isn't working the way it should. Instead of seeing my thirty-year-old self they are seeing the sixty-plus persona who has colonised my body, and I mutter a silent apology to my parents' generation for writing them off.

That generation seemed much older and so many of them died young. Compared to later generations, they lived in dangerous times. Service in the Second World War was certainly a health hazard. My father-in-law and stepfather both came home with no visible injuries, but their health had been compromised in different ways by their war service. My mother and stepfather married a few years after his wife died of a cancer, which today has good treatment outcomes, and after my father died in a road accident. My stepfather then died at sixty-two. As cars became affordable and my parents' generation embraced motor vehicle ownership, cars became a significant killer. A seatbelt would have stopped Dad being thrown out of the car on his head. He was one of 2,534 people to die on the roads in 1962. He was forty-two and the population of Australia was ten point seven million people – now it is around twenty-three million, and the rate of car ownership is much higher.

The national road toll, which now includes cyclists and pedestrians, has been more than halved and is declining.

Words for medical conditions have been an unwelcome addition to my vocabulary as I have become older. Consider the word 'infarction'. I first heard it in the waiting room of an intensive care unit and my first instinct was to laugh. If ever there was a word tailor-made to describe devastation to the human body, this is it. There was no laughing as the surgeon told my husband's family their mum and my mother-in-law would die within hours because of an 'infarction of the small bowel'. The surgeon explained the artery to her small bowel had become like a water pipe blocked up with silt. A colostomy bag could not fix it; there was no replacement part. It was a privilege to be at that bedside vigil as Edie told us how much she loved us.

Despite this, I was not prepared for the impact of the word 'lymphoma' or its finer shades of meaning. My father-in-law seemed to wander in a wilderness of shock before his condition was diagnosed. Within twelve weeks of my mother-in-law's death, he died in palliative care. He was a sign writer and painter, and I had watched him wash his hands in turpentine many times. My husband and I wondered how much of his disease could be attributed to environmental factors, and whether he would have done anything about it if he had known the risks. I was in my early fifties and took stock. In the midst of suffering, sometimes there are worse things than dying.

Life is more precious and it is easier to be grateful once you realise you aren't invincible. Like me, friends of my age are facing up to – or facing down – their genetic inheritance and doing what they can to ameliorate it. The range of common conditions we are managing probably fits neatly into a statistical paradigm: arthritis, diabetes, hearing loss, cataracts, glaucoma, occasional memory lapses, prostate problems, heart conditions, susceptibility to cancers and mental illness. The image of the Grim Reaper in the bowling alley from the AIDS prevention advertisements of the 1980s comes to mind when I think of a friend battling MND (motor neuron disease) and the Parkinson's disease that my husband has lived with for some years. We all make more effort to catch up. We make adjustments and laugh more; none of us are giving in.

Lynsey and Lynn, Munich

'Retirement' is not a word we have adopted as a lifestyle. Having held down jobs, raised families and paid off mortgages, many of us now have the freedom to be what we wanted to be when we grew up. We are working, often for love rather than money. We provide hours of volunteer labour for clubs, societies, charities and younger or older members of our families. We have embraced the online world, but are well represented in the numbers of people who develop relationships with shop assistants and purchase goods in bricks and mortar stores. Savvy marketers have realised they ignore us at their peril. The image of the doddery and senile in God's waiting room is not a fit for us.

Hey, Paul,

Don't forget to apply for your Seniors Card. Free public transport in Victoria on weekends and much more. Maybe you will be challenged by the transit police. 'Come on, son, you don't look old enough to be a senior!' Don't hold your breath. The kids who serve at our bottle shops are sick of us asking why they don't ask us for proof of age. Deep down we know that they admire us for buying bottles instead of casks. See you at the party.

THE THIRD THIRD

JOHN BENNETT

'Life is not a dress rehearsal.' These words from a friend kept coming back to me as I entered my fifty-fifth year on the planet and my thirty-seventh year in the employ of the Commonwealth Government. There was a similar message in the wisdom of our middle daughter, many years ago, when we were on a houseboat on the River Murray. She warned her younger brother, 'If that water rat over there by that willow tree bites you, you'll be dead for life!'

Elizabeth, wife of many years, had resigned her paid job some years earlier so she could follow her other several passions. The National Gallery in Canberra trained her for twelve months so she could be a gallery guide. She undertook a post-graduate diploma in art history at the Australian National University and found a piano teacher who would guide her towards the agony and the ecstasy of piano playing and the attendant exams, left behind some forty years ago.

Was I to die at my Government desk? Surely that was not my goal. But there was a problem. I liked my job. It was interesting and it paid relatively well. The workplace wanted me to stay. I had good health – how long would that last?

Would I have enough money to do the 'other things' I wanted to do when they stopped paying me every fortnight?

But life is not a dress rehearsal. Bite the bullet – just do it. So I did.

That was twenty years ago. What is there to show for it?

In Elizabeth's case several half open doors appeared. She pushed them open and went through. Like Alice in Wonderland – and sometimes with similar chaotic and surprising adventures. One example of what can be found on the other side of the door comes from her volunteer guiding at the National Gallery. Although working with and enjoying the total gallery collection, Elizabeth developed a particular interest in Indigenous art. Leading a study group to assist guides better understand Aboriginal and Torres Strait Islander art led to many satisfying outcomes and many unforgettable moments.

How else would one find oneself sitting in a dry creek bed at Ernabella in far northern South Australia watching an Aboriginal play.

Or getting geographically confused in North East Arnhem Land as darkness falls, only to be 'rescued' by locals in the area.

Or wading safely about one hundred metres to a small boat near the Coburg Peninsula, finding out afterwards how quickly crocodiles can travel.

Or attending North East Arnhem Land's Garma Festival and working out how to return from the toilet block and re-find your own tent in the darkness without waking all the neighbours living in the hundreds of identical tents, neatly in rows.

Or meet mask-makers, headdress-makers, model-makers, linocut artists and ghostnet weavers in their own space, doing their own thing and telling you how and why.

Or, after three annual visits, have friends on six islands dotted

Preparations for a Torres Strait islands ride

through the Torres Strait between Queensland and New Guinea who are happy to see us again.

Other doors, or opportunities, also asked to be opened because we were available. I joined the local community garden and within

Archaeological digs

days found myself the Garden Convener (for a two-year stint) because no one else would take it on. I soon found out why.

I (willingly) accepted a request to help tend an area near where we live which was being revegetated. Some of 'my' trees are still alive! Many though were kangaroo and wallaby survival food during the long drought.

We joined a volunteer program with the University of Sydney on an archaeological dig in Pella in Jordan for three weeks. Would we have been digging up Bronze Age artefacts or Roman shards if we had stayed in Canberra? Or sitting down with fellow volunteers in the evening to see the sun set across the desert?

And let's not forget the children, grandchildren and even great-grandchildren. Occasional child-minding, introductory trips to the Art Gallery, football games and education (for us!) in the mysteries of the digital age. I haven't mentioned pottery and family history research and photography and community bike rides and visiting interstate rellies and friends. That will have to wait until we've got more time.

So, to date, our superannuation is still keeping us going financially and our bodies are holding up (just). As someone said, 'If we wake up one morning with no aches and pains we will rejoice in the fact that we have died and gone to Heaven!'

Are we enjoying the third third of our lives? Of course, but speaking of the chances of reaching the magic ninety seem pretty slim! Maybe the actuaries and their statistical tables are wrong.

So we reckon we should keep on going for now, today and tomorrow. The space we have been in is too good, too easy, awesome, and above all deadly!

And when we're dead, we're dead.

GIVING OF ONE'S SELF

LOUISE VAN DER VELDEN

I retired from the workforce just after my sixtieth birthday in the year 2000.

My job involved working by appointment and I was forever chasing the clock. Although I enjoyed my job, I felt that there were other things I wanted to pursue, such as study, craft, establishing new friendships with women, etc. and I became aware of perhaps having limited time to indulge. I also wanted to get involved in community work as a volunteer, particularly in supporting women with breast cancer.

I am a long-time breast cancer survivor (1980) and after undergoing a mastectomy with chemotherapy follow-up, I felt that I could contribute something after this experience. I decided to follow the Lifeline study course where I learnt many skills. The training was brilliant, but I found that telephone counselling wasn't really 'my thing'. I prefer to have face-to-face contact with people. I then contacted several organisations involved in cancer issues and palliative care.

At one hospice where I went once a week for six months I spent time with patients listening if they felt like talking, or otherwise just sitting with them. I found this quite a rewarding experience.

However, it was at another organisation where I found my niche.

It was a holistic, not-for-profit facility offering support through counselling, courses, complementary care, support groups, etc. Originally I was offered voluntary work one day a week, performing administrative duties and telephone support.

After a few months I was asked to co-facilitate a small support group for women with cancer. In the days when I was diagnosed there was little or no support for women with breast cancer, as it was quite rare to be diagnosed as such.

Of course we now know how things have changed and many women and some men are diagnosed each year with this disease. The current facilitator was retiring and the idea was for me to take over the group. My Lifeline training came in very handy and I found it a very rewarding experience to be part of this group where women were able to be authentic with each other as to how they were coping, and more importantly, how they were feeling. I found that as the group grew in numbers that there was wonderful support in sharing between the women.

The opportunity for studying to become a counsellor was offered to me after a few months, which I gladly accepted, even though the study required attending weekly meetings, some weekends and lots of assignments. But I completed the course and I believe that it contributed to my role as group facilitator.

During the ten years that I spent in this organisation I attended a number of forums and national conferences, and met some wonderful people, health professionals, etc. I have learnt many skills and received much satisfaction from my working in a voluntary capacity.

While there, I became involved with a group of ten breast cancer survivors. Together we have attended several retreats over the years and have developed a very strong friendship and support for each other. We meet for four hours once a month at each other's home, and have a theme which is nominated by the person at whose home we meet. Last year we celebrated our ten years together and it looks like it will continue for many years to come!

I had also been interested in some sort of craft and through a chance meeting with a very talented and creative woman I became interested in quilting and patchwork. She has become a lovely friend and I have learned much from her and the workshops I have attended.

Together we visit exhibitions, craft fairs, etc. She is also my movie buddy! I have completed many quilts for family and friends and have developed an interest in designing! The sky is the limit!

After a very busy working life I feel very happy to have time to develop friendships with other women, and I now have several really good friends. I do believe friendship needs to be worked on from both sides in order to prosper.

Grandma and granddaughter

I'm very aware that in our circle of friends, health is a constant issue, and during the past fourteen years there have been some challenging times regarding the health of myself and my husband. So far we have been able to cope.

I practise yoga every morning and try to meditate regularly. I find that it assists with living in the 21st century! My other indulgence is reading! I love books and read every day.

My husband has always been very supportive in whatever I have wanted to do since retirement. We both have separate interests, but also do things together. We delivered Meals on Wheels for eight years, and really enjoyed it. I believe you have to find a certain balance in your life in order to be content.

I am grateful for every day of my life. We are blessed with two wonderful children and two lovely granddaughters and we are expecting our first great-grandchild in April this year.

I count my blessings, of which there are many.

My final comment: to give of yourself to others is the most rewarding experience and a real privilege.

SEVENTY-TWO AND STILL GOING STRONG

GLENN REES

In 2000, at fifty-eight years of age, I was fortunate to start a new chapter of my working life.

My dream of heading up a major Commonwealth Department was gone. I had been told, as a consequence of leaning too far towards the interests of the Aboriginal and Torres Strait Islander Commission during the ongoing tensions with the Government of the day, there was no future for me.

The advice was that 'sliding doors' provide new opportunities – go and find them! My wife and daughters celebrated the fact that I would be leaving the Aboriginal and Torres Strait Islander Commission and a very difficult and stressful working environment. I was not allowed to sense any feeling of failure.

I was faced with the agonising decision about whether to simply retire, take up a consultancy of some kind or look for a job. It was my wife, of course, who found the solution in an advertisement for the position of Chief Executive Officer of Alzheimer's Australia.

It gave me new hope, not least because I had enjoyed my time working on the reform of aged care between 1985 and 1993.

I was offered the position with the suggestion that before accepting I inspect my new office that was part of an old child care centre shared with the Alzheimer's Australia ACT organisation!

It transpired that the national organisation had been dysfunctional for a couple of years. There had been no website, no policy publications for many years, very limited and insecure Government funding, and the Queensland organisation had left the Federation.

In a strange way, this was all refreshing. Not to have a budget of $1.5 billion and all the staffing headaches that go with it was almost therapeutic. To sit and think and plot a strategy for the future was fun. And I could rely on the Alzheimer's Australia ACT organisation with its strong consumer focus and happy atmosphere to keep me honest.

The then Minister for Ageing, Bronwyn Bishop, kept to her promise in June 2000 that if Alzheimer's Australia got its act together nationally then she would support new three-year contracts and increased funding for Living with Memory Loss programs, dementia training and other support services including the dementia helpline.

This was the start any Chief Executive Officer would dream of in their first three months. The decisions coincided with a summit of Alzheimer's Australia stakeholders from across the country at Melbourne University in June 2000. The dream of making dementia a national health priority was born.

In my lonely (heavenly) office I was left free to plot a strategy that might result in dementia gaining a higher policy profile. As luck would have it, Professor Tony Jorm, then at the Australian National University, wrote a publication for me explaining perhaps as succinctly and brilliantly as anyone why dementia is one of the biggest health problems facing Australia. It was published in 2001 at an Alzheimer's Australia board meeting in Adelaide.

To my surprise, we had every national television station come out to the offices of Alzheimer's Australia South Australia to interview me on the publication. I discovered that dementia was of interest to the media and their audiences, and more importantly that to attract the media you need not only talk about the problem but the solution.

Dementia initiatives

The challenge became one of finding economists who would risk their reputation in trying to measure the economic and social impacts of dementia and strategies for the future. Access Economics were prepared to take up the challenge and in March 2003 Alzheimer's Australia released perhaps the most seminal of all our publications in the last fifteen years, 'The Dementia Epidemic: Economic impact and positive solutions for Australia'.

It caught the imagination of politicians in high places and a commitment was made by the Coalition during the October 2004 election to implement the Dementia Initiative: Making Dementia a Health Priority. This commitment came with substantial additional funding that was honoured in the 2005 Budget of $320 million over five years.

In personal terms, my work enabled me to do what I love, which is trying to translate complex policy ideas and evidence into policy and programs. And most importantly to adopt a consumer focus in all our work and develop strong consumer networks. There is perhaps nothing more exciting, at least in my view, than combining thinking and doing in the area of social policy with consumer involvement.

The work I was doing kept me in touch with many of the people I had enjoyed working with in the 1980s and early 90s on aged care. There were so many new networks in terms of clinicians and researchers prepared to do so much valuable pro bono work for Alzheimer's Australia, which was heartening to say the least.

So many new publications and initiatives flowed from this work. Perhaps among the most important was the commitment that Alzheimer's Australia made to consumer-directed models of care where it is the consumer who takes decisions on services that best meet their needs and when, where and how they should be delivered.

The opportunities in this area were immense. I had the pleasure of working with Jane Tilly from the United States drawing together a publication on consumer-directed care and whether it was a direction for Australia.

Then there was the opportunity to work again with Warwick Bruen, an offer, which I deeply valued in personal terms, and was seminal to eventually persuading Government to adopt consumer-directed care in new packages. Warwick, on retirement, volunteered to come and work with Alzheimer's Australia. A magic moment was when an advisory group to the Minister decided that a recommendation would be made to adopt consumer-directed care and Warwick turned to me and said, 'We've done it!' I was glad that he was able to see, before he died, progress in the dream he had to ensure that community services would be made more responsive to the needs of individuals.

Many publications followed on issues as diverse as dementia and sexuality; LGBTI (Lesbian, Gay and Bisexual Transgender Institute) communities and dementia; advanced care planning; palliative care; dementia risk reduction; the quality of residential care, and issues around physical and medical restraint.

If the 2005 Budget had been a turning point in the recognition of dementia as a priority, so too were the decisions taken by the then Government in 2012 on the Aged Care Reforms. It had been a real battle for Alzheimer's Australia to get dementia recognised as a serious issue that had to be tackled in its own right in aged care, and that mainstream care simply wouldn't do the job.

Under the leadership of Ita Buttrose, the then President of Alzheimer's Australia, we adopted a high profile Fight Dementia Campaign including a march on Parliament House in Canberra in October 2011 and vigorous use of social and conventional media.

The icing on the cake has been the decision in recent times to make $200 million available for dementia research over five years. This is something that we have been advocating for since 2002 and which more recently formed a key element of the Fight Dementia Campaign.

If keeping physically, mentally and socially active is an important part of positive ageing, my work has pushed me to do all of these over fifteen years including tackling the challenge of ensuring that the Federation was seamless in its presentation to the wider community, politicians and media.

I feel so fortunate that there was a sliding door, that my wife spotted it, and that I have had a wonderful fifteen years leading a great organisation to pursue the interests of its consumer stakeholders. It has been a wonderful journey with the support of our State and Territory members and boards who have been prepared to promote the change in an organisation from a conservative to a much higher profile in its advocacy and use of media. Receiving the honour of Member of the Order of Australia (AM) in 2013 was an unexpected recognition of all that I had achieved over these years.

If there is a regret, it is that some of the skills that I have learnt in my sixties were not acquired much younger in life! The use of the internet and email have changed the workplace out of all recognition and there has been the challenge of coming to terms with skills in new areas such as media and fundraising.

I stepped down as Chief Executive Officer of Alzheimer's Australia in December 2014 and took up a voluntary position as the Chair of Alzheimer's Disease International and, if time allows, will do some consultancy. I hope that some of the new skills I have acquired in recent years – including media – will translate to the international level.

I am now seventy-two, and if my seventies are as enjoyable as my sixties, I will feel more than fortunate that I decided not to retire when I was fifty-eight.

I RIDE A BIKE

IAN LITTLE

My name is Ian. I am a MAMIL. That's my confession. I am a 'Middle Aged Man In Lycra'. I ride a bicycle. Not just down to the shops and back to get the bread and milk. MAMILs don't do that mundane stuff, not wearing lycra anyway. I regularly cycle sixty to eighty kilometres, preferably in the hills. Perhaps as I am sixty-nine years old, I should really call myself an OMIL, an 'Old Man In Lycra'. But you are only as young as you feel, so I am sticking with calling myself a MAMIL. (Political correctness prevents me from quoting Groucho Marx at this point.)

I want to share with you some of the favourite bike rides I have done over the last few years.

I am fortunate to live in Surrey Hills, one of Melbourne's leafy eastern suburbs. This is a one hour ride from the Dandenong Ranges. There are many roads through the Dandenongs. My favourite I call the world's greatest bike ride. This is not bragging – it is! Starting from Belgrave the route takes a steady climb through the tall eucalypt forest to Kallista, then an exhilarating plunge through broad curves before a short uphill to Monbulk. Onward to Emerald, the forest is more open and the corners tighter, to the valley floor where tree ferns flourish. Riding through the valley on the smooth bitumen is a slow ride to take in magnificent scenery with the early morning sun filtering through the gums.

The conversation is predictable with snippets of 'Isn't this great' and 'Aren't we lucky to have such a great place to ride so close to home'. The sting in the tail of this ride is the climb up into Emerald, but the reward is a great morning tea at the Emerald bakery. Then it is nearly downhill all the way back to Belgrave through Puffing Billy country, crossing the track several times, going under the famous trestle bridge and a short climb into Belgrave.

Touring overseas on a bike allows a whole new way to see the world. I have ridden in France (several times), Italy, Spain Switzerland and Vietnam. Because you travel slowly you see so much more. You are in the scenery and life, not just viewing it through a window. The bike gives you the mobility to look around a small town and ride up and down its streets in minutes when it would take all day on foot.

For about twenty years, a group, which includes some of our closest friends, has been making a pilgrimage around the wineries of Rutherglen. Early on this spawned the idea of touring overseas. So we did it. And again, and again, and more to come. For me the highlight of these trips was our tour of Vietnam. There seems to be only one road rule in Vietnam – maintain a steady course avoiding other people and don't do anything unpredictably or suddenly. If you want a true adrenalin rush I recommend going for a bike ride with thousands of locals during peak hour in Hanoi. It is a unique way to meet the people.

Le Tour, the Tour de France, is an amazing sporting event to watch on TV. To see it for real is part of cycling heaven. In 2010 I went on a cycling tour following Le Tour for a week. The highlight of the trip was riding on the course a few hours before the peloton – the group of professional racers – charged through.

We set off from Lourdes on a warm sunny morning along the rail trail in the river valley to Argelès-Gazost. Here we turned onto the road to start the fifteen-kilometre climb of the Solour. People were lined up along the roadside for the whole route with their picnic tables and chairs. I suspect there was more than a little wine drunk to pass the time as they waited at their selected vantage points to see the peloton stream by later in the day.

We riders provided the entertainment before the main event, Le Tour peloton. Spectators cheered us along with calls of 'Allez, allez' as we climbed up at a snail's pace. On particularly steep pinches, spectators would enthusiastically run along giving a push. All well intended, but a bit alarming due to the unsteady state of the 'helpers'.

At the top of the climb we settled and waited for the peloton. Just as in the TV series MASH when the whir of helicopters signals incoming wounded, for Le Tour spectators the arrival of helicopters signals the arrival of the peloton. This was fascinating as the helicopters came upwards from the valley below. The crowd chaos on the road was even more hectic than it appears on TV – if that is possible. It all passes quickly; the peloton flashes by, being no more than a blur. Many questions of 'Did you see so-and-so?' all with the same answer 'No!' The ride down the mountain completed the spectacular adventure; freewheeling and picking a path through pedestrians wandering aimlessly all over the road along with swarms of other cyclists. Everyone excited and elated having seen the gladiators of Le Tour.

I had to cut short my 2010 Tour de France tour as my wife became ill and I had to fly out. This left some unfinished business. There were mountains not climbed. So the following year I organised my own tour of the French Alps and Pyrenees with a mate of mine. I can proudly boast of having climbed some of the iconic climbs of Le Tour including Alpe d'Huez, Col du Tourmalet, Solour/Aubisque, Ornon, Les Deux Alpes, Col du Lautaret and Galibier. The highlight was the Col du Galibier climb. This was a forty-four-kilometre climb from our guesthouse, called Le Velo Jaune, near the base of Alpe d'Huez. We set off on a clear sunny day not that confident we were up to the challenge. My personal goal really was to get to the Col du Lautaret, the pass where the road heads to Italy. This would miss the steepest nine kilometres of the climb but still have the long return ride home through the valley. On TV I had watched Cadel Evans fly down this valley chasing Andy Schleck in the 2011 Tour de France and just wanted to do my own Evans' impersonation.

Cycling alongside the Volga, Russia

We were feeling good after three hours riding when we stopped at Col du Lautaret for our standard cycling lunch of a ham and cheese breadstick with black tea. So we headed on. The higher we got the steeper the road became, stepping up to eight to nine per cent gradient for the next nine kilometres to the Galibier tunnel entrance. At this point there is a tall monument to Dr Henri Desgrange, the first director of Le Tour. We had a passer-by take our photo in front of the monument and I was ready to head down. We had the evidence that we had done Galibier. My attention was drawn to a road still going up. So after being bribed with a Mars bar I put my helmet back on and we rode the steepest section. One kilometre and a 150-metre climb later we really were at the saddle of the Galibier at a height of 2650 metres. Standing in the small car park perched on a ridge I stood in awe of the view, and our achievement, and wondered how they ever managed to have a stage finish of Le Tour in such a small area. Five-and-a-half hours to climb up, one hour to fly down. That says it all.

I grew up on a farm in the rolling hills of South Gippsland, about ten miles out of Korumburra in Victoria. I had always thought it was good country, but I never really appreciated it until I went on a bike ride with my nephew, Bruce Car, which included a visit to the farm on which I had grown up at Bena. We went on a 100 km loop ride from Wonthaggi to Korumburra and return. This took us through Glen Alvie, Jumbunna, Korumburra, Bena, past my home farm on the way to Kongwak and returning to Wonthaggi via Lance Creek. Good quality sealed roads with little traffic through green rolling hills with outstanding views from the ridges.

In 2014 I went on a tour of Switzerland with a group from Whitehorse Cyclists (the largest cycle club in Melbourne). As we cycled along the magnificent trails in the flat eastern cantons, the rolling hills reminded me of South Gippsland. The Swiss scenery was stunning, but South Gippsland provides us with comparable views and riding right on our doorstep.

In closing, I must debunk the image I hope you have built of me as a super athlete who has ridden a bike since he was five years old. *Au contraire mes amis*. Truth is I am a geriatric, visually impaired asthmatic who started riding in my early fifties. (I had ridden my first bike in the fifties.) Geriatric: sixty-eight years' worth and aiming to keep counting. Asthmatic: diminished lung function due to several bouts of pneumonia. Visually impaired: have not driven a car for thirty years, colour blind, corrected vision about five in twenty (You may see it at twenty metres. I will see it at five metres, if I see it at all). This provides challenges of being unable to read road signs and spot hazards. Getting lost is not a disaster, bumping into things is not so good. My personal research has led me to a theory that if a person on a bike hits something at a speed greater than twenty km/hr, bones will be broken.

Fortunately the ageing cyclist demographic is a supportive lot. I take to the roads early every Sunday morning with a group of like-minded blokes in Surrey Hills. We travel in all directions. We all enjoy the exercise and the resultant wellbeing and mateship. I am a follower, even when I am the ride leader who has nominated the route for the day. I attempt to follow about five metres behind a rider. Any closer and I may fail to slow down or brake and hit the bike in front. Any further back I may miss the sign or call. It is not uncommon for me to react too slowly and respond with 'Yep, hit it'. This support with signalling and calling warnings allows me to see the world from a front row seat, the bicycle saddle. As Ringo Starr sang in the popular Beatles song 'I get by with a little help from my friends'.

BIOGRAPHY: A RETIREMENT PROJECT

BETH DUNCAN

I found life on a small farm in the Adelaide Hills, following an early retirement from social work, very different, but non-the-less busy and rewarding; as also was the opportunity for engagement with the local Hill's community. Volunteering during the Ash Wednesday bushfires of 1983 led to my becoming the inaugural editor of the district newsletter, *The Voice.* Working as a volunteer social worker for a local youth hostel also took a slice of time, and I always looked forward to my weekly day trip to Adelaide to work in the newly formed Volunteer Centre.

Downsizing with the sale of the farm and a move to a town house in Adelaide was another major change, although we retained our holiday home at Clayton on the lower Murray as a retreat. George, my husband, who had driven down to Adelaide three and sometimes four days each week to work, really appreciated the reduction in driving time from an hour, often through fog in the winter, to one of a few minutes.

We loved the proximity to the cinemas and particularly the theatre and took out a subscription each year for the State Theatre's season. It was also great fun to absorb the energy and excitement and to participate in Adelaide Festivals, Writers' Weeks and Cabaret Festivals.

However, I still had time on my hands and, as a beginner, joined a croquet club that had courts in the parklands only a short walk from home. I eventually became Club Secretary and then President, but never a good croquet player! A writing group also beckoned and as my interest in writing developed I enrolled in and completed the Advanced Diploma in Professional Writing at the Adelaide College of TAFE. As a result I began research for a biography of an early pioneer.

Mary Thomas, in November 1836, was one of the first white women to reach the new colony of South Australia, even before Governor Hindmarsh had arrived. With her husband Robert, and four of their five children, she was off-loaded from the *Africaine* into whale boats and then landed, with other settlers, onto the beach at Holdfast Bay. From there they made their way on foot through sandhills and scrub to set up camp at a site near what we now call the Old Gum Tree. The Thomases had a very happy reunion with their eldest son Robert George, aged 16, who was already in the colony as an apprentice with Colonel Light's survey teams.

The Thomases bought land in Hindley Street, now a main street in the city of Adelaide, and moved there to make a base for their home and business. They had migrated from London, from their prosperous Fleet Street printing works, to set up a printing business in Adelaide and to publish Adelaide's first newspaper. It became very well known as the *Register*. Ownership was to continue in the Thomas family through William Kyffin, the Thomas's second son and then his sons, for almost one hundred years. The Thomas's association with *The Register* meant that they were close to, very well informed about, and sometimes quite influential in, the major events of the time. Mary Thomas was a well educated woman and, alongside Robert, her work on the paper in the early years was invaluable.

Born in Southampton, Mary died in 1875 at the age of 87, having spent thirty-nine years in the colony, all of them in Adelaide. She witnessed Adelaide's development from a clearing in the bush, to a significant town with its streets graced by beautiful churches – such as the Flinders Street Baptist Church and Pilgrim Church, designed by her eldest son, Robert, who had trained as an architect – as well as civic buildings such as the Town Hall and General Post Office. Their construction had been supervised by Robert George Thomas while colonial architect-in-chief.

One of the most enjoyable aspects of writing the biography of Mary Thomas was the research involved, which extended over about five years. There were many letters, diaries, and family papers to read and study, as well as the numerous issues of *The Register* newspaper covering the period of Mary's life in Adelaide. I fitted the research in between regular visits to Sydney during school holidays to look after two granddaughters, and visits from them for beach holidays. I also accompanied George on many of his trips to Asia during his years as a consultant for an international firm.

Research led me to Southampton of the late 18th and early 19th century to gain an understanding of the environment in which Mary grew up. It was the era of the French Revolution and of the wars with France, when the people of Southampton suffered the constant threat of invasion. Research into life in London following Mary's marriage in 1818 until her departure for South Australia in 1836 gave me an appreciation of how women of Mary's social class managed their homes and families and the types of amenity Mary left behind in migrating to a new, raw colony.

My knowledge of English history of this period had been very sketchy, and I was generally enriched by this new knowledge. Similarly research into Mary's later life in South Australia greatly increased my awareness of the privations and hardships the early colonists confronted, of the political climate in which they found themselves, which was frequently fractious, and of the often unpredictable aberrations of the economic cycle. At the personal level, Mary's diaries and letters and those of her daughters provided invaluable insights into life in an Adelaide middle class family of the era and the ways in which they managed the consequences of disastrous economic downturns.

Although the research was often a slow grind requiring determination and commitment, it was seminal to the writing of the biography. Its spin-off was a greatly enhanced appreciation of early South Australian history.

Some of Mary's descendants, who were my contemporaries, provided invaluable assistance in the research. They invited me to work in their homes and gave me access to personal family papers, and insight into family recollections of Mary. Many have become firm friends. Working together we were able to compile a list of names of a sizeable portion of Mary's descendants, now spread throughout Australia. My new friends and I organised a family gathering to launch the biography following its publication by Wakefield Press. As well as South Australia they came from Queensland, NSW, Victoria and Western Australia, representing descendants of each of Mary and Robert's five children. It was the first time they'd had a family gathering and the first opportunity most had of meeting and getting to know the individual stories of their fellow descendants. As you can imagine there was much excited talk, much laughter and many reminiscences. I was delighted and touched to be invited to become an honorary member of the family.

A few years later when the West Terrace Cemetery Authority included the gravesite of Mary and Robert Thomas in their tour of heritage graves, it became apparent that the Thomases' grave was badly in need of restoration. Heartened by the enthusiasm with which the earlier gathering had embraced their family story and heritage, a small group of descendants decided to take action. They invited me to join them in undertaking the restoration of the gravesite. It was through contacts made at the previous family dinner that a list of descendants was drawn up and approached to request their support.

Launching the biography

The response was overwhelmingly positive and over the next two years, while technical and heritage matters were being sorted out with the West Terrace Cemetery Authority, they were kept in touch with progress. When permission was given for the reconstruction to proceed, the supporters were canvassed for funds. It took only a matter of months for the very significant funds required to be donated, and the contract for the work let. The project was finalised in February 2014 with a gathering of donors, many from interstate, for the blessing of the reconstructed gravesite. The service was conducted by one of Mary's descendants, a priest, who had come especially from Western Australia, and who fittingly used the prayers which would have been used in Mary's day. A family gathering for morning tea ensued, with again much excited talk, laughter and many reminiscences.

One further spin-off from the biography was the opportunity to brush-up and hone my public speaking skills. Women's groups in particular expressed interest in Mary's story. Over the years since the biography was published I have had frequent requests to address Probus, Penguin, Legacy and women's literary clubs, as well as historical societies. It has always been a pleasure to meet members of these organisations, to learn something of their activities, and to hear their own stories of pioneer ancestors.

As a kind of off-shoot from these talks, and with the help of two actor friends, for several years during History Month, we conducted walks around areas of Glenelg which would have been well-known to Mary Thomas and other early settlers. We developed a script in which the actors read from the diaries of Mary Thomas and other fellow pioneers quoting their descriptions of the environment of Holdfast Bay as they had experienced it. We stopped at various significant points along the way for the readings, with morning tea, fittingly, in the *Buffalo* café and we completed the walk at the Old Gum Tree.

My interest in history (particularly of South Australia) and in writing continues to enrich my retirement years. As a volunteer I have been involved with a number of projects for the Glenelg Historical Society and the Holdfast Bay History Centre, and continue to give talks on aspects of these projects.

LIFE IN THE SIXTIES: LIFE WITHOUT ENCUMBRANCES

MALCOLM COWAN

At around sixty years of age I started to see my life in a different way. When you are young life is something that seems to stretch from childhood to who knows where and your view of old people that they were born that way – how could they have ever been young? Things happen to change your perspective. It may be an event or a combination of triggers. It could be lower family and financial commitments, an opinion you hear, some learning you undertake, a lecture or book that changes your view of the world or produces an 'ah ha' moment, but whatever it is you start seeing life through different paradigms.

My view of my future life span has changed. A significant event for me was the death of my father at the age of 89 after an active and healthy life. Dad's death brought it home to me that I was now at the front of the family queue inexorably moving towards the cliff face from which we all inevitably drop off. The deaths of friends and people your own age also become the norm rather than the exception. Deaths and disabilities generate a fear of loss of independence or a prolonged life without reason or enjoyment.

There is now no far off horizon but a more specific timeframe and it's a timeframe I can relate to because I have already lived that span – I have a feel for what fifteen or twenty years means.

Now in my sixties, I can also put the longer historical time span in perspective. The whole timeframe of my life so far has been the same as that from before the Boer War to when I was born. In 1948 the social and political repercussions of World War 2 were still resonating through Australia and the rest of the world.

Significantly, in my sixties, my wife Vicky helped me realise that we have choices that we can make about how we live our lives and our attitude towards life. For example, to various degrees depending on personal circumstances, we can choose to take some responsibility for our own health and well-being by eating well and keeping active. We both ride bikes and have taken up long distance bike touring in our sixties. We use our bikes for local transport and recreational riding and spend as long as four months at a time cycle touring with our tent around Asia or Europe. I play tennis with a group of friends, ski and swim with a club. I do some occasional work in a bike shop and we have a large vegetable garden.

Cycle touring in Asia and Europe

Vicky rides regularly and does aqua fit classes and we both do Pilates. We are members of a reciprocal hosting network for bike tourers which brings us into contact with like-minded people from around the world through summer. I am actively engaged in our Tamar Bicycle Users Group, fostering and advocating for greater bicycle use and running group rides. We might not live any longer but we feel mentally and physically better, and hopefully we can improve the quality of our later lives.

Mentally, we can choose the outlook we take towards life and other people; choosing whether to be trusting and open-hearted, optimistic and positive or, conversely, suspicious and distrusting, pessimistic and negative. Unfortunately it is easier to be negative and conservative rather than open and questioning, particularly in the current political adversarial world and what we now have confirmed about the catastrophic effects that our changing climate will have for our children and grandchildren. While there is still a population and politicians in denial and opposition from vested interests, being enthusiastic is hard work. I also have feelings of guilt about not doing enough to help change attitudes on significant social issues such as climate change or asylum seekers.

Slipping into gloom, doom and grumpiness is easy, but it doesn't make for a happy life! So we try to develop circles of like-minded, positive, active and supportive friends. Life is too short to be bothered with the others – and at least we can do in our own backyard as we would like the rest of the world to do in theirs.

Vicky has a successful small business, Vix Kitch, producing jams and chutneys that we both sell at the Harvest Farmers' Market. Saturdays at the market are part of our social life as we greet our regular customers and meet new ones, and generally have fun interacting with people – jams with attitude!

I had a career in the Department of Primary Industry and then left to start my own consulting business when I was fifty-two. It wasn't the best decision financially but mentally it was healthier than staying in an organisation that was changing radically from the one I'd joined thirteen years earlier. The only challenges became how to find the next round of budget savings.

Looking back, self-employment gave me a wide range of project experiences, some quite stressful because of the steep learning curves I was launched into; but generally it was very satisfying. This gave me a diversity of experiences dealing with different people and businesses and an insight into many of them. This also generated a number of frustrations, apart from the normal ones of physical ageing. I've seen a wide range of alternative careers that would have been very satisfying. We need a 'rewind' button to have another go at those. If I were starting again I would be making a career in bicycle training and advocacy, or maybe freight logistics or event management or maybe even a theatrical set builder. Or perhaps we would have started a farm tourism venture. Transitioning out of conventional work is important; I gradually gave up full-time work over three years as outside interests gained higher priority.

As I've aged I think my tolerance levels have changed. I have gathered wisdom and become more tolerant of people's foibles. I appreciate the wonderful kaleidoscope that is humanity, but I have become less tolerant of self-promoting idiots with big egos! In my wide experience I have unfortunately seen a lot of people with inflated egos making decisions in positions way above and beyond their abilities and without the life experience needed to make good judgements. A mule in a suit is still a mule.

Now I am free from the daily round of conventional work and family responsibilities, it seems that I have more time to be aware and interested in broader political and social matters. Earlier I was too busy to be aware and involved in local issues. Now I realise that it's the local issues that are important and affect our daily quality of life more than most of the higher level politics. Local issues are about the livability of the city, the environment in which people can interact with each other. We have seen the farmers' market transform the social life of Launceston on Saturday mornings.

On a local level there is the chance to actually become involved and change things, whereas at the national level we have the frustration of being isolated from the decisions and the decision-makers and their lack of long-term strategic thinking and action. Decisions are made on the basis of the political election and twenty-four-hour media cycles, arrogantly claiming wide mandates on the basis of electoral campaigns in which none of the issues were ever presented to or evaluated by the electorate.

With the locals

One of the many benefits of teetering on the edge of being 'over the hill' is that you do have a view both in retrospect and into the future. We can see where we have come from and how we got there. Australia is a very different country from that when I was growing up. Then we had strong links to the land, particularly through relatives or friends on the Soldier Settlement farms. We have lost these country/city links.

There was also sense of nation-building, with major infrastructure projects and forging a place on the world stage. We have become more multicultural, a process that was not always one we embraced – remember the 'wogs' and 'dagoes'? And although locally we are generous and supportive, nationally we have lost the natural sharing and sense of fairness and equality I remember as we have developed a 'me' based value structure.

My generation of baby boomers has lived through one of the most affluent periods in history and we have become accustomed to unsustainably high standards of living. Our parents' values of thrift and abhorrence of waste have been lost in a wallow of self-satisfaction, high expectations and over-servicing; none of which have been shown to make us any happier or healthier. Our travels overseas slowly on bicycles have shown us that (while of course not denying the need to raise health and living standards) some of the happiest and most generous people we meet are the people who have the least. Fortunately there are some wake-up calls sounding and many in our younger generations are changing behaviour patterns so there is hope and good reason for optimism.

Travelling has also reinforced how important is a sense of community. It's the natural state rather than isolation but we have allowed our urban structures and lifestyle to shift us away from a village setting. We are trying to develop our immediate neighbourhood as a community and we are working towards a wider sense of society through involvement in local issues. I now have time to write the occasional letter to the editor of the regional daily newspaper.

I encourage people to evaluate their working environment regularly; are you happy and are you diversifying your lifestyle and circles of friends outside work? If you aren't enjoying it – give it up or find something else, perhaps volunteering. You don't need as much money as you think you do and as they say, no one on their deathbed has said 'I wish I'd spent more time at work'. I'm finding my sixties to be a very happy and fulfilling time in my life.

Do in your own backyard as you'd like the rest of the world to do in theirs!

RIVER CHANGE: TOM AND ROSEMARY'S STORY

ROSEMARY BUILDER

Retirement was not a word acknowledged in our vocabulary in 1989, despite the fact that both my husband Tom and I were nearing our sixtieth year. After working together for twenty years in our own businesses, with our marriage still very much intact, and our four children independent in the wider world, it seemed irrelevant, until –

With a twenty-year-old cruiser resting in a local marina at some expense and, not wishing to experience another rough Lake Alexandrina crossing to reach the calmer waters of the Upper Murray, we had already begun to look for a riverfront property to give us our own mooring and camping site. An old boatie sent us a Riverland paper advertising the auction of a 'historic site' on the Murray River between Morgan and Waikerie. 'Too far', we said, 'but let's go and have a look anyway'.

Look we did. We fell in love with the view and a vision of what could be. We bid for it successfully, thereby changing our life direction dramatically. The 'historic site' consisted of three buildings, one basic rectangular building, the second a half cellar and the third a large barn, all built of local sandstone embedded with fossilised shells from a sea world long past.

Previous readings of the *River Murray Pilot* had not alerted us to the fact that the site was recorded as a 'RUIN'! The twenty-acre block itself appeared just as neglected and unloved as the buildings, being covered in a mix of saltbush, introduced weeds such as the once medicinal horehound and Dutch caltrop; all doing their best to disguise years of farm and hotel rubbish.

The Inn before restoration

Hotel? Yes, hotel, we were told in knowing terms by the locals who were no doubt thinking, 'Stupid townies, paid too much for it of course!' But already the knowledge that it was built in 1860 and had become the next stagecoach stop west of the Overland Corner pub, was welding us to a project of restoration to last for the next ten years.

To make this possible was to disencumber ourselves from all of our business activities and property in Victor Harbor as soon as possible. By 1991 this was achieved and the property was habitable enough to move up and away from the last twenty-seven years of very happy child rearing, project adventures, town involvement; all of which had created many friendships – a huge amount to leave. But it was time to go.

The two years between the purchase and final move were a very special time – a time of challenge, yet of fun and physical effort – on which my visionary Tom had always thrived. Our instigator, Boatie Bill, was installed as caretaker with his stout companion, fox terrier Daisie. His first task – a condition to my first sleeping in the house – was to seal all cracks and crannies that might admit a snake or two or more. (A previous brown visitor had already been dispatched in a bedroom!)

Bill's previous experience in the building trade was invaluable as there were many other repairs – the half cellar being a priority – to which he could put his skill to work; as long as there was a relaxing glass of port at the end of the day.

After the first shock of our purchase, our family and some very special friends were caught up in the challenge, joining us for weekends on a camping basis as facilities were very basic. Owing to a ten-kilometre gap in the grid, there was no electric power. There was however an adequate gas stove and 'modern' toilet to serve our most urgent needs.

Luxury

In the heat of the River summer an old bath and shower stand were found in the rubbish and set up at a water pipe outlet, in full view of the road. It became a dangerous distraction to passing motorists, the level of distraction depending on the age, sex and discretion of the bather! After a hard day's work it was a luxury leading up to a very Happy Hour around the campfire and barbecue before dossing down on swags or mattresses.

Work inside included repair to white ant-eaten floorboards, followed by sanding and polishing. The old pub cellar was discovered and found to be full of plaster dumped in the 1940s when the hotel interior had been changed into a family residence.

An image of our oldest daughter emerging from the underground with buckets of plaster and literally white as a ghost will never leave my memory!

Outside a young fruit salad orchard was found competing with head high weeds, all of which were removed with gusto. The Morgan Elderly Citizens gathered up truckloads of rubbish from which they could earn funds. A huge bonfire was the answer to non-recyclable rubbish, and resulted in an emergency call out for the Cadell Country Fire Service, many of whose members were offenders and therefore inmates of Cadell Training Centre. They were very disgusted to find the fire well under control, with no risk to the area and their 'escape' curtailed.

Not long after moving into the house permanently, we were both offered positions in Berri: Tom to establish the first Tourism and Travel Course in TAFE, and I as a co-ordinator with the Intellectual Disabilities Service. Although it was an hour's travel up and back each day, we were both thrilled to use our previous experience and qualifications to take on this new challenge. And of course the salaries assisted us to finance further restoration.

It was time to call in the tradies. The starkness of the house was softened by a curved veranda, the bolts for which had been inserted in the walls in the forties, but the cost of finishing them was unaffordable. Piece by piece we painstakingly planted Santa Anna couch lawn around the building after having spread many loads of river sand and grape waste or marc from the wineries. The local builder, who provided the excess lawn cuttings, regrouted stone walls, including those of the barn after it was restructured with steel and galvanised roofing. The barn's interior walls had their graffiti censored with fresh plaster, the floor was paved with bricks and three pine-walled bedrooms erected.

A recycled kitchen completed the open living area for what was intended to become self-catering accommodation for travellers. It was a far cry from its history as hotel stable, shearing shed, chook house and local dance venue, the last use ended by fire ... Yet we were able to retain the mallee shearing stands and fill the wall exits with glass tiling. An ablution block was built separately but connected by a breezeway.

Furnishings in both buildings were also designed to retain their history, but by necessity gas and solar power had to replace the candles and lanterns. Water was pumped from the underground tank dug five metres deep out of solid limestone a hundred years before – and after a drowned snake had been removed! Cosmetic touches were added with a terrace garden to the south and a rose wall to the north, plus what every late Victorian garden always had – a fern house and an herb garden.

By the time Tom and I eventually in 2000 came to build a new house on another part of the property, also with a grand view, the property was unrecognisable from 1989. The locals remarked what a bargain we had bought and how they should have put in a bid!

Our eldest son and family had joined us, establishing an accredited organic orchard and Mallyons Bush Café and Gallery, named after the licensee for twenty-three years from 1862 – William Mallyon.

But the 180-degree view with its ancient river and gracious river red gums is still the same, with the ghosts of the Overlanders leading their cattle down to the flat named after Harry Weston, the first pastoralist there. And also of the timber cutters providing fuel for the paddle-steamers and living hardily in timber huts and dugouts in the side of the gullies and at risk of summer storm and flood.

You may just hear the rumble of the coach arriving from Overland Corner at 11 pm to be greeted by the Brand daughters kept awake, they say, with a tipple of port; the noisy arrival of the Governor and his retinue for the annual race meet on the track to the north of the hotel; brawling in the bar resulting in blood on the floor. You may also hear of the mystery skeleton discovered without identity in the bush not far inland but where it is still so easy to be lost. No, not young Henry Bryan who travelled with explorer Sturt. But who?

It is all still there in this very special place discovered by us at a very special time.

KEEPING THINGS WORKING

DAVID BENNETT

In a daze, having just woken from unconsciousness, I struggled to get up from the bitumen bike track. My old road bike was on top of me, the length of my left side grazed and bleeding and my helmet split in three places. Later in hospital I discovered my pelvis was broken in two places as well.

Was this supposed to happen to a seventy-two-year-old who was riding most days just to keep fit and to enjoy the outdoors? No but it's a risk one has to take.

It was really no more than a little setback, albeit one that took more than twelve weeks of pain and physio to overcome. I'm back on the bike again and holding the handlebars a little tighter around the corners.

I had ridden a bike most of my childhood (heavy steel bikes with no gears) and then for many years to work. This latest riding phase is for fitness and pleasure. It's easier and more enjoyable than the jogging I used to do and much of the riding is to prepare for mass participation community rides such as at the Tour Down Under Challenge, Amy's Ride and Velo Adelaide. I choose the options anywhere from 60 to 100 kilometres each.

And when you are training, it helps to live near Adelaide's River Torrens Linear Park which has a bike path stretching for 30 kilometres from the foothills, through the city and down to the beach. Then there's a pretty steep bike path up the Old Mt Barker Road to the top of Mount Lofty to really get the heart rate up.

I was nervous at my first fun-ride attempt in 2011 riding on the same road as 7000 other cyclists, many of whom think they are in the Tour de France, but its success gave me more confidence to continue on other rides. What has been really pleasing is that now members of the family from 11 years old to 76 years old have got the bug and we all regularly compete together in these fun rides. Over the past four years my legs have pedalled close to 10,000 kilometres. Hopefully there are another 10,000 left in the old legs yet.

As well as riding around on bikes as a child we spent many great holidays on the River Murray camping and fishing and maybe this led to a couple of other activities undertaken recently by me and my wife Ellen.

A friend of ours, Pearl Wallace, was Australia's first female river boat captain. She was born into a riverboat family, grew up on paddle-steamers and then herself captained paddle-steamers on the Murray. A first for a woman! Part-time throughout six years, over many cups of tea and enjoying Pearl's delicious scones, we listened to and taped her story and made it into a book which was eventually published. Her life, not so remarkable for her, was fascinating to us and now it is recorded for posterity. The trips to various river towns selling the book, meeting new people and seeing lovely places were great experiences.

The book gave us the bug to seek out more interesting river stories. This led to interviews of twelve of the long-term older residents of the Murray River town of Morgan over a period of two years. Their oral history interviews were recorded on a tape recorder. Interviewees' first reactions were, 'I'm not going to talk while that microphone is pointing at me!' Some quiet and

Holding a next generation rider

reassuring chat from Ellen would soon change that fear and once the microphone was forgotten the fascinating stories would come flowing. We heard from fishermen, pastoralists, teachers, woodcutters, council workers, charcoal makers, fruit growers and more. A kaleidoscope of roles that went to make up the river towns of yesteryear. Then we heard of the common threads binding people together such as floods, droughts, long distances, poverty, sickness, war, coming of the railway, death of the river trade and emergence of the motor vehicle. All of the photos our new-found friends had of their lives were scanned and arranged in a slide show to accompany the recorded interview. Both interview and photos were put onto DVD. These are now a permanent part of the varied exhibitions in the Landseer Museum in Morgan.

Caring for others features strongly in this phase of our lives. Firstly there were three years of looking after Ellen's mum, living in our own home.

While her memory of the last hour or day might have faded quickly, such that she would say to Ellen at around 5.30 pm each work day, 'That tall man's coming in the back gate with his bike again', it was always a delight to hear those clearer memories of exploits from many years ago. The companionship of a gentle soul who said that every cup of tea was the best one she had ever tasted and us never having to find an elusive sock to put with its mate, because our mother sat quietly organising them in pairs for us, was reward enough for the constant attention that her care required.

From looking after a person at the end of her life to caring for another at the beginning of his, three mornings a week, it's now up early for both of us. 'Tad' and 'Grandi' head down to our three-year-old grandson's, to look after him while his mother goes to work and his dad sleeps until the afternoon after a long, cold, night-shift job.

What great fun, anxious moments and absolutely delightful experiences with him. By now he knows every playground in the area, where to catch the train into town or down to the beach and where to get an ice cream or chips from the many cafés in the area. On two of the mornings it's off to play group and a dance and song group, 'Shimmies'. It's non-stop physical and mental exercise each day.

After all this what's for relaxation? Creating and tending to a community garden plot just over the river from where we live. Just a few square metres, but at the moment it is 'chock-a-block' with spinach, silver beet, broad beans, tomatoes, rhubarb, sweet peas and a healthy windbreak of peppinos. Not forgetting the white butterflies. It's a learning experience too. Finding out how to organise an Esther Deans 'no-dig' garden, listening to the other growers and generally experimenting each season.

Grandson in the community garden

It's another activity where we share the experience with our grandchildren and share the results with family and friends.

How do these disparate activities, riding bikes, writing books, producing DVDs, looking after aged parents, young grandsons and growing vegies relate? They are the total package. Together they provide both physical and mental sustenance and a meaning for these advancing years.

It is just as well we don't have full-time jobs because we would never have the time otherwise. The sad thing is that we had to wait for over sixty years or more for all these interesting activities to invade our lives. Let's hope that rather than killing us they sustain us for many years to come. We just have to stay on the bike, be one step ahead of the grandson and avoid the odd brown snake in the garden plot.

LETTING ONE'S IMAGINATION SOAR

MOIRA McGEE

When couples in the United Kingdom retire, they often move to a little bungalow at the seaside. We were already living at the seaside so we moved to Australia. If you have to move, do it properly!

It wasn't a whim on our part as we had lived in South Australia before – in the late sixties, early seventies. My husband was in the RAF and was sent from England to Maralinga, South Australia, for a thirteen month tour of duty. We had no children then so I followed him, found a flat and a job, and waited for his posting to end. This way we saw one another every couple of months or so. We were hoping to extend our stay in Australia by having him seconded to the RAAF Base at Edinburgh in Adelaide – and this came to be.

We were given temporary quarters initially, then a service house in Elizabeth South. Our first child was born, and we loved life in Australia. When my husband's time here ended after four years we fully intended to return, but it didn't happen that way. It was late 1998 before I returned.

I have connections to Australia over a long period. My grandfather moved to Queensland with his eldest son, Peter, in 1930 and worked in the apple orchards. He is buried in Ipswich. His youngest daughter, my godmother, moved to Sydney with her husband in 1939 and had three children. Peter had two children. So, I had Australian aunts, uncles and cousins. It was wonderful to meet them; we weren't like strangers, they felt like old friends.

When I returned to Australia at the end of 1998 I was given a four year visa. My husband remained behind to sell our home and all belongings and finish up at his job. By the time he arrived in 1999 the rules had changed and he could only have a six month visa. This meant he had to leave again after six months. We went to the Immigration Department to find out what to do. As we had sold up in the UK we had nowhere to return to, which made our whole plan seem like a damp squib.

I'll gloss over the following ten years it took us to become Australian citizens.

As my eldest daughter is an Australian citizen she bought a house as an investment and we lived in it and paid the bills. At the time of our arrival she was working in Japan but had to return to Adelaide for two years in order to sponsor us. We weren't allowed to work. I felt it was such a waste of our talents so we volunteered to work at our local hospital; one shift in the kiosk selling food, coffees etc. and one shift taking a trolley of newspapers, magazines and sweets around the wards. My husband's health wasn't too good after a time and he stopped, but I continued at the kiosk for about nine years.

I saw a notice in the local paper asking people to volunteer to teach English to immigrants. I applied and completed the nine-week course. I began with one-on-one students, then moved to a TAFE college in Salisbury which I enjoyed very much. Through both of these jobs I have made many friends and continue to keep in touch with them on a regular basis.

Ten years ago I had a Vietnamese student, a young married lady with four children, and we are good friends to this day. I have met many members of their extended family, been invited to socials at their church, two family weddings and various parties. I have had an insight into their way of life, culture and cooking I could never have envisioned.

With my students

My husband and I have mined for opals in Andamooka, travelled to Sydney several times and been to the Head of the Bight to see the whales. We have visited Alice Springs, Uluru and all around that area. We had a great week in the Flinders Ranges, explored the rainforest in Victoria and visited many small country towns in NSW, Victoria and South Australia. We have been to Melbourne, travelled the Great Ocean Road, explored Geelong and all along that coastline. And I wouldn't dream of leaving out the wonderful wine regions of South Australia. We have had a most interesting twelve years of holidays, travel, social outings and friendships.

The one sad note for me was the death of my husband at the end of 2011.

I still have a great circle of friends, and will continue to enlarge the group. I belong to a quilting club, two line dancing groups, an exercise class, a monthly social outing group and a writing group. Next month my writing group is having a book launch. We present short stories and poems contributed by many members of the club including myself. Until a few years ago I had only written essays for school and letters to friends, but now I can let my imagination soar. It is so rewarding!

Reaching what is supposed to be the last stage of one's life is only boring and difficult if you allow that to happen to you. I have often wondered if we did the right thing by coming to Australia so late in our lives. I don't think you ever forget the country of your birth but we have embraced living here and have had many visitors from Europe over the years. It has been fun showing them around and comparing our way of life to theirs and thinking of all the regrets we might have had if we hadn't taken that huge leap but stayed safe and predictable in our little retirement bungalow by the sea in the United Kingdom.

PLANK WALKING

PETER LUMB

I'm not sure what I've done since I turned sixty because I can't exactly remember turning sixty. I can remember that my birthday has always been on 16 December, and on that day of every year in Australia, as a nation we wilt. We're exhausted by what we have done over the year, and we have the certain knowledge that we must celebrate Christmas and we then must be exhausted and sociable all at once. So no one, with the exception of my good wife, Fiona, remembers my birthday on 16 December. I lack a marker for the passing of the years. That's the truth!

The story of 16 December and the period of my life in the run-up to what I imagine was my sixtieth must be told if we are to make sense of life after sixty (a bit of comparative analysis). I worked in a university most of my life pre-sixty (so I've marked a lot of essays). And in the years prior to turning sixty I was exhausted more so than the usual pre-16 annual kind of exhaustion. I could no longer fake being diligent, constructive in my essay-marking comments and more or less cheerful. I had to see a counsellor.

Visiting this counsellor, 'my counsellor' as I now want to refer to her, was the pivotal activity in my truthful story about what I've done since (roughly) achieving sixty years. My beginning story to her was that I was exhausted. I loved my job, I did not start superannuation contributions until they became compulsory and I was a bit short of funds, so I needed help to manage my exhausted days at the university through to sixty-five at least. There was another reason I could not leave the university, but which I could not initially say out loud to my counsellor, and that was I knew with certainty no one else would employ me. Summer and autumn had disappeared from my life and my seasons were study periods one to seven, and one graduation ceremony each year. I was an entrenched academic with no prospect beyond the tower. So, the question was, how could I manage at the university for the years between my counselling sessions and sixty-five?

That story to my counsellor changed pretty quickly to 'OK, I'm about to be sixty, I'm exhausted, pasty looking, more rotund than I have ever been, unfit, no one will employ me, but I'm leaving the university anyway.' So begins my true story of life since sixty. I was jumping into the abyss, walking the plank, facing the future blindfolded ... I resigned.

At the very moment (!) of resignation my daughter living in Bondi gave birth to our first grandchild and Fiona coincidentally located a small apartment for two in Bondi, for three months. And at the very next moment a Swedish academic and his family wanted to rent our home in Adelaide. We said 'Yes, we'll have the grandson, the Bondi apartment and the rent money', and soon after I was sleeping in each morning in Bondi before wandering off to nurse the baby. I was bleary-eyed to begin with but all was joy! My advice is that once you've turned sixty, rent an apartment *and* have a grandson in Bondi (but not too close to the backpackers along Campbell Parade).

Just as I was sufficiently alert to notice the whales disappearing and the frangipanis blooming outside my favourite coffee shop in Fletcher Street, I visited the Art Gallery of NSW, where a second pivotal moment occurred. I was enjoying the Australian colonial art when my phone rang and I was offered a contract consultancy in a government department, in Adelaide. I was rude and told them I was enjoying the von Mueller in the NSW Gallery, I was still recovering from my work disease, I had a grandson to love, and I was in Bondi. Goodbye. An hour later in the Contemporary Collection the phone rang again. Would you like to work part-time? When would it suit you to begin? Would you like to negotiate a pay rate in this range? They outlined attractive tasks which I knew I could do. I said, 'Thank you, I'll ring you back in a week.'

Bondi grandson

I was no longer exhausted, I had a beautiful new grandson who magically reached out to me, and I had work four days a week with the promise of no night or weekend work finishing after 7.35 hours of work each day, plus super.

Well, work has gone on from there. I became a sole trader. I acquired an Australian Business Number (ABN) and public liability insurance. I learned how to write an invoice and a friend steered me into the consultancy business. I worked short and long contracts. When contracts finished in say November, then there was nothing on offer till late January the next year – a lovely long holiday. I seemed to adapt to uncertainty pretty readily.

During that first long contract after Bondi I discovered that public servants almost always work hard, but once every so often there was a birthday to celebrate. We'd all gather in a small crowded room for morning tea, drink coffee, eat cake and tell weak jokes at which everyone laughed. We'd all contribute to the word Target from the *Advertiser* newspaper and after twenty-five minutes the room emptied. There were complaints about bureaucratic routines at times, and I complained about the lack of autonomy, as you'd expect from an ex-academic, but generally people got on with each other, enjoyed their work and kept reasonable hours. They did not look exhausted to me. This was an important revelation and I went home and described the coffee and cake parties in detail to an astounded Fiona. At university we had electric jugs in our individual offices and drank instant black coffee alone.

And so it went. I found I had sought-after skills which were applied to other work. I could do social research. I could pull together long reports to send off to Canberra. I could process those submissions the public contribute to government departments. I was sent off for training and learnt how to write ministerials, I enjoyed a range of activities and worked with people with diverse skills. Post sixty I was learning so much. I was stimulated and doing significant work. I felt valued.

When I turned sixty and retired from my long career, friends who'd arrived there before me advised me to plan my transition, rather than to wait and see what happened. Being convinced I had poor paid work prospects, and that I mostly lived in Adelaide without grandchildren, I began to volunteer. I trained as a bush carer, I joined the board of an organisation and I joined the committee which organises the almost annual Australian Walking and Cycling Conference in Adelaide. Bush care is flexible volunteering but my other activities are less flexible. In part I set up these activities as a hedge against too much idleness, social isolation and attention deficit syndrome. At times it has been demanding managing my subsequent paid and unpaid responsibilities but I've had the pleasure of working with many admirable volunteers and have enjoyed the diverse activities so much.

At sixty Fiona and I moved from the suburbs to the city. We left our attractive, large 1880s crumbling suburban villa for an almost new city townhouse with no cracks, drafts, extensive garden or maintenance needs. Longer commutes became short walks to the various city offices where I worked. I lost weight. Maybe the move from a demanding home to an undemanding one also cheered me up. I love city life. I don't experience traffic congestion, and endless talk about car parking is none of my business. This is a different and engaging life style.

I walked the plank *and* jumped into the deep (while my counsellor stood on the deck smiling encouragingly) prior to the Global Financial Crisis. During and after the GFC I was paid by State and Commonwealth departments when there was money to stimulate the economy as well as me. I was privileged to work on projects associated with the Living Murray Program, and with AusAid in Indonesia and Adelaide. There are less opportunities today. I was fortunate in the timing of my sixtieth.

When I turned sixty I found a counsellor, a grandson (there are now two dear boys, by the way, and still in Sydney), an apartment in Bondi, significant part-time work, and city living. My mostly satisfying long-term career ended. There were a few difficult currents and unseen reefs along the way but right now Fiona and I continue our travels (often to Sydney); we're enjoying the Adelaide Fringe and a few Festival shows with our friends; and I'm planning to ride my bicycle off-road to McLaren Vale with friends. This is my first year of not expecting to do paid work. I'm sixty-seven and pretty fit and managing those little aches and pains.

RETIREMENT: THE BEST JOB WE'VE EVER HAD

NORIEL NOBLE

My husband, John, retired in 1994 and I continued to work part-time till 2002 and the extra money earned allowed us to indulge our passion for travel in Australia and overseas.

John always was a handyman and never found any trouble finding jobs to do around the family home and at our three children's houses. He also was involved with Neighbourhood Watch and was the editor of the local news-sheet for many years. At a meeting of the Neighborhood Watch the speaker from the council talked about volunteer workers to help elderly people with their gardens and control of graffiti within the council area. The graffiti removal had groups of people of four or five to a vehicle, with a supply of different coloured paints and special solutions that could be used to remove graffiti from signs and walls. If it could not be removed it would be painted over. He had to give this work away when he had a hip replacement, but then found the golf club needed a volunteer to assist with the computer operations on the match committee. This kept him busy three days a week for seven years.

I have always been involved with the church, in the choir, women's fellowship and on the church council, but when I retired from work I needed something else to give me an interest. So I applied to be a volunteer at the Adelaide Festival Centre, and was trained as a tour group leader showing visitors round the complex, explaining the special features in the four theatres, the dressing rooms and function rooms and the large art collection. I also play tennis every Tuesday morning but I am starting to realise that my tennis days are numbered.

A volunteer grower for fifteen years

I was a Trees for Life volunteer for fifteen years and helped the environment by growing over 5000 seedlings for South Australian landholders. All the trees were grown from seed and nurtured almost daily, watering and making sure that at least one seedling was growing in each tube.

Always having something in the future to look forward to is really important. We realise we must keep fit and healthy to be able to do what we have planned.

John's involvement in target rifle shooting meant travelling throughout South Australia and to all states in Australia, New Zealand, Bisley in the UK and Bloemfontein in South Africa.

We try to go away somewhere different every year. I must say our bucket list is getting shorter, but we still find places to go to. We have already planned a couple of cruises for January the year after next.

One place that was on top of our bucket list was Machu Picchu in South America

Overseas together

In 2005 we flew to Santiago in Chile for a couple of days, then flew to Lima in Peru. From here we travelled up into the mountains to a lodge at the top end of the Amazon River system. It was a real experience; no electricity, long drop toilets, cold showers, hot and humid. It was a great contrast to our normal five star hotels. There were wild animals and birds everywhere. Children would appear with a monkey or sloth around their necks. Beautiful coloured friendly macaws would land on the railings around our rooms. We were taken to the Yagua Indian village and had a demonstration of how to use a blow gun. Then onto Cusco to see the Inca Ruins with the marvellous stone work where no mortar is used and the rocks were shaped to fit perfectly into each other.

Finally we arrived at the magnificent Machu Picchu ruins; really an amazing place.

We visited the Uros Indians on Lake Titicaca. They had built their reed homes on reed floating islands to give them safety from attack.

Next to Rio de Janeiro to have a swim on Copacabana beach and to see the remarkable statue of Christ the Redeemer, another wonderful structure built in 1930. Travelling on we went to Argentina's spectacular Iguassu Falls. We have seen the waterfalls in other places but this one left all the others in its wake. We went out on the steel walkways built fifty centimetres above where the water tumbles over the top of the falls, then later climbing down to the bottom of the falls to travel in small boats to the throat of the falls with the water spray and mist drenching us.

The tour was for five weeks and we were lucky to have a wonderful group of travelling companions from most Australian States. We have had a reunion nearly every year since, each time in a different State. Our last reunion (2015) was held in Melbourne and this allowed us to have a tour of the Melbourne Cricket Ground (one of our bucket list items).

In 2010 one of our daughters announced she was going to have her fiftieth birthday dinner on the Eiffel Tower on 20 June 2012 and asked that we all come over to join her. Trying to find reasonably priced accommodation in Paris for eight people (Lucy, her sister, her daughter, her mother, plus partners) was a challenge!

We found there was a ship (the *Athena*) leaving from Perth going around the bottom of Africa to Southampton. This was going to be a few weeks early for the birthday party, so we found a river cruise from Budapest to Amsterdam that included a coach to Paris and three days in a good hotel.

The river cruise with Scenic was very well organised, the meals were silver service and we had magnificent views as we travelled on the Danube, Rhine and Rhone rivers to Amsterdam. We then travelled by bus to Paris via Belgium with a lunch stop in Antwerp.

Paris lived up to expectations. With visits to Versailles, the Louvre, Monet's garden, a night bus and boat tour and the meals on the Eiffel Tower, all made more enjoyable by having most of our family with us. It was a wonderful holiday.

In the Blue Lagoon thermal pool

In July 2014 we went off again, this time to Copenhagen and cruised to Iceland via Norway, Shetland Islands, Faroe Islands, and Kristiansand in Norway then back to Copenhagen. Of the 600 passengers on the ship over half were American and we made some new good friends.

We had a daytrip from Reykjavik in Iceland to the Blue Lagoon. The water was beautiful and warm, about forty degrees in the water while it was only six degrees outside.

In Copenhagen we stayed on the ship, and just moved cabins for the second cruise. We sailed to Edinburgh, where it was wet, cold and very busy with the Tattoo, Festival and Fringe. Being a golfer John wanted to go to the 'home of golf', St Andrews, so we did a coach tour. It was wet and cold at St Andrews but the golfers dressed in their winter woollies continued to hit off on the first tee at their allotted time. Then we sailed round the top of Scotland to the home of the Beatles, Liverpool, Holyhead in Wales, Dublin in Ireland, Isles of Scilly, Dartmouth (where we visited the summer home of Agatha Christie and were most impressed), followed by the Channel Islands, then to Southampton and on to London. We really enjoyed the couple of days in London, where we went to see *Les Miserables* and travelled on the Hop On Hop Off bus – a great, cheap way to see large cities.

We really enjoy cruising. In 2010 we unpacked once and for 104 days sailed round the world Sydney to Sydney. It was wonderful. The accommodation, food, entertainment every night, and the service from the crew was first class. On each cruise we meet a new group of people from all over the world.

GIVE, LIVE AND LOVE

JANET NICHOLSON

'Yes you have cancer', said my surgeon. I was then twenty-seven, my son was three and my daughter eight months old. This event changed my life.

I am now nearing seventy and have learnt much in the intervening years. I am grateful for the life I have, and make the most of every day. Cancer really confronts you with your mortality and helps to define what is really important in life – family, friends, being there for them, making the most of every moment, seizing opportunities, taking on new challenges, learning from failures, forgiving and ... so much more.

In my sixties, life is good. Maybe it is the 'getting of wisdom', accepting who you are 'warts and all' and accepting that we all make mistakes. The important thing is learning from these – the lessons of life.

This decade has heralded a lot of changes. For example, for sixteen years I had worked in a senior management position in a large Commonwealth organisation. When I was sixty, I decided it was time to do something different, but was unsure what this would be. I needed to work but at what/where? So I resigned after sixteen years in a permanent, secure, and senior position. I was asked many times by work colleagues 'why are you leaving, where are you going and what are you going to do?' My answer? It was time to do something different, to be challenged rather than stay on and be comfortable.

So I left, with no job security, with only a three-month contract to work in the Kimberley as a family healing support worker with Aboriginal communities. What a change that was – the outback/the last frontier, flying in light aircraft to work in remote communities as an on-the-ground front-line worker. I learned a lot and hopefully contributed to those with whom I had the privilege of working – smoking ceremonies, community problem solving, the challenges of few services and cobbling together whatever services existed ... and there weren't many. This fuelled my commitment to doing what I could to provide the best service I could for those living in remote areas.

After the three-month contract? Well, I have never been out of work and have been fortunate to have had amazing work opportunities coming my way – working across the Northern Territory as a staff counsellor that afforded me the opportunity to work with many dedicated people, seeing the most hauntingly beautiful and spectacular scenery, learning to drive a 4WD, travelling on dirt roads, changing flat tyres and driving long distances without seeing another person. I also worked in child protection, sadly an area of high need but it fitted with my commitment of trying to make a difference, however small, in the lives of children.

I learnt what a wonderful country Australia is – the scenery in many of these places is awe-inspiring and the people are so generous. I remember working in Alice Springs when the bushfires were raging in Victoria and the generosity of spirit of those living in 'The Alice' was truly inspiring. Three semi-trailer loads of goods were quickly dispatched and fund-raisers organised – a true demonstration of the Aussie spirit – helping those in need, asking for no recognition, just wanting to help out.

Work is but one aspect of my life. My family is very important to me. After working in regional/remote Australia for three years it was time to return home, not just every six weeks or so (and *always* for Christmas, Easter and for family birthdays), but to come home for good.

I came home to help out with grandchildren, to work to help my family financially, as well as having fun times with the grandchildren. Dressing up as a lion to perform in our make-believe circus and coping with the bemused look of the handyman who had come to do some work around the house; to be the wicked witch at Halloween; to organise the Easter egg treasure hunt; read stories; be the tickle monster; a dare devil at the playground, and babysit!

What am I doing right now? I am still working full-time, moving from working in the area of brain injury to working with families where there are child protection concerns. I enjoy my work and the opportunity it provides to continue to try to make a difference in the lives of children and also their parents. Being a parent, particularly a single parent (I have been there) can be a real struggle and children don't come into this world with a 'how to do it' text book. We often learn through making mistakes, so I try to learn from life's lessons and wisdom gained in helping others.

Travel continues to be a passion and my grandchildren (I have four who are the joy of my life) often ask if there is somewhere in the world I haven't been! Historical and archaeological sites, England, Europe, particularly France (and the food), are favourites along with the wilds of South and Central America.

Six months ago I went on my own to Northern Peru for ten days to see remote sites, accessible via a ten-hour overnight bus

In Northern Peru

trip and difficult climbs (certainly for this almost seventy-year-old). The death-defying walks along narrow paths with sheer drops, and steep climbs were features, along with the experience of riding a horse to visit a remote waterfall, clinging to the horse led by a sprightly woman who was my age, wiry, fit and wearing a large white Stetson hat.

That trip highlighted for me the way I live my life – embracing the unknown, living for the moment, being positive and enjoying whatever life has to offer, accepting the good, the bad and at times the ugly moments in life, never losing faith and continuing to learn, thinking of others and above all to be there for my children.

'Give, live and love' is my guiding principle.

VOLUNTEERING: A NEW CHAPTER IN OUR LIFE BEGINS

CHRIS GRAHAM

I have been volunteering at Trinder Park Resthome for the past nine years. Volunteering means the world to me.

Having worked hard all my life from the age of twelve until sixty-five years, I became a mother, grandmother and great-grandmother. Once my family had all grown up and left home and was not needing my help any more, I needed something to fill in my time and keep my mind busy. So I became a volunteer to help the elderly.

I began to volunteer at Trinder Park because my mother was a resident there. I visited her daily and got to know the other residents and enjoyed helping out with their lifestyle activities. After her passing I could not walk away from Trinder Park, as I could see that helping the elderly gave me a purpose in my life and there is no better purpose then helping the elderly. One day we will be in the same position.

I find just as much enjoyment visiting and helping the elderly as they do. I find it very rewarding. Over the years I have helped set up a lovely garden area for family and friends to use which I call 'Mum's Garden'. Now my husband also comes and helps me to care for this garden. Last year I was nominated for 'Logan Seniors of the Year Award' in recognition for all my years of volunteering at Trinder Park. I was very surprised and thrilled to receive this award.

Last year we decided to sell the family home and purchase a small three-bedroom home in the grounds of Trinder Park. Finding myself with even more time on my hands I increased my volunteering hours at Trinder Park. As well as helping the Diversional Therapist, Janet, in the high-care area to run activities ranging from morning teas, craft and cooking groups and even bus trips, I took on the role of running a card group for the Resthome Area. This group meets once a week for about two-and-a-half hours. We design and make cards so that everybody in the facility can receive a handmade card on their birthday. We have even started making get well cards for those who are not well. The group started off with only four people attending. Now we have up to twelve people each week, making over one hundred cards.

Since moving to Trinder Park I have also become involved in helping to keep the cottage residents socially active. I run a craft group every Wednesday afternoon where a group of ladies gets together to make craft items for the upcoming fete. I also help with the line dancing on a Friday morning, and my husband and I help run the weekly swimming group and monthly bus trips.

My advice to anyone who is retired and looking for something to do is to go and find yourself a volunteer role that you love.

THE FIRST SIXTY YEARS ARE JUST A WARM-UP

RUDY VAN ACKER

Born in 1940/1939, my wife Dorothy and I have always been reasonably active in our married life. We have owner-built three houses and renovated two, with some prospects of moving again.

When the youngest of our three children was three years old, we started travelling in a small fold-out camping trailer during two week annual leave periods twice a year to inland NSW, Queensland and Victoria. Our two girls had ponies when we lived on various acreages, so we were involved with Pony Club events for a number of years.

From 1980 onwards I became involved with the NSW Rural Fire Brigade some distance inland from Port Macquarie, assisting with equipment maintenance and fighting bushfires. After moving from the countryside to suburbia in Kempsey in 1988, I joined the State Emergency Service assisting during flood events in the Macleay River valley. Over a number of years, using river level and rainfall data, I developed a system of predicting when critical low-level river crossings would become inundated, as many homes could be isolated for up to a week.

In 1996 we travelled for nine weeks around the UK and Europe in a rental motorhome, enjoying the different cultures and meeting

Emergency services

many friendly people, some of whom wanted to practise their English on us. On return to Australia we bought a Toyota Coaster bus partially converted to a motorhome, as we wanted to camp independently instead of using on-site vans. Attending a number of large Campervan and Motorhome Club of Australia (CMCA) and Chapter rallies in New South Wales, Queensland and South Australia we met many members and obtained plenty of ideas to assist in completing our additions/alterations.

Having retired from part-time work in 2000 we moved to Wingello, a small village in the Southern Highlands of NSW. Whilst camping on-site in our motorhome we built a separate garage and a large steel-framed house with our granny flat, joined to a previously relocated army barracks. Aided by Dorothy, and two of our children as well as five grand-kids, this was completed at the end of 2001 just in time to celebrate Christmas dinner with the whole family at a very large table.

Unfortunately, the 'Sydney Fires' started that afternoon and having earlier joined the local Bushfire Brigade, I was fighting fires for the next fortnight and hardly home. Early in 2002 we 'escaped' for eight months to travel anti-clockwise around Australia attending major CMCA rallies at Barcaldine (Queensland) and Northam (West Australia), visiting numerous towns, going on local tours and some flights to see interesting places. Since about 400 motorhomes went 'Over the Top' we kept running into many of the same friends, travelling together for some time before parting ways to check out different destinations. We followed the WA coast around the bottom and in SA stopped at Ceduna to observe the total solar eclipse in early December – awe inspiring.

Back home in Wingello we established raised vegetable garden beds and planted fruit trees as well as flowering ones. In 2003 the youngest daughter and son-in-law, with five grandchildren, went to Georgia in the USA for two-and-a-half years to work. We visited them for three months to assist with a newborn grandchild as well as travelling around the area when things settled down.

On one memorable trip we camped in State Parks along the Blue Ridge Parkway well into Virginia, using a seven seater vehicle with rear seats removed and an inflatable double airbed installed. It was very primitive but really enjoyable. We met many friendly American country folk, who wanted to keep talking to us just to hear our accent!

We continued on to Holland to visit my aunt and cousins in Ymuiden near Amsterdam, renting a car for six weeks to explore many areas around the country, as I was only thirteen years old when the family migrated to Australia. Periodically we came back for a rest at my aunt's place, before departing to visit other places, staying at bed-and-breakfasts, Youth Hostels or occasionally a hotel.

To complete the stopping-off requirements of our 'Around the World' air ticket, we visited many highlights in Singapore for a week before returning to Wingello.

In the following years we attended more Campervan rallies (one in Tasmania), and fought bushfires in Victoria and ACT. We kept on growing vegetables, many being used in the local general store/post office/take-away that our daughter and husband had purchased on their return from the USA.

There are many minor repairs to be carried out, as our son-in-law isn't a handyman, although he is very good as a business advisor and computerised accounting systems installer.

More grandchildren arrived here (now eight in total) and since they have all been home-schooled we have had our hands full over the years with requests for assistance to 'fix this or that', 'show me how to crochet or knit', 'help me make this' or 'can we go for a walk through the bush?'.

Our eldest daughter and son, both living and working in Canberra, periodically need assistance as well.

In 2006 we bought a larger bus to convert into a motorhome, complete with island double bed, convenient kitchen, bathroom, solar panels, fresh water and waste-water storage tanks, so that we could camp away from caravan parks and be totally self-sufficient. In the period of its conversion to the end of 2013 we travelled in the old Coaster for periods up to five months during winter to the warmer areas of Queensland, either by ourselves or accompanied by friends. Seaforth near Mackay is one popular destination as we have made many friends there, some of whom come regularly from as far as Tasmania.

On completion, the new bus went on its maiden voyage to Tasmania for four months to visit Dorothy's sister for Christmas, as well as friends made over the years whilst travelling around the

Conversion under way

mainland. My brother and his wife came over in their unit and we accompanied them for a fortnight. On return to the mainland we visited Western Victoria, attending a major CMCA rally at Robinvale on the Murray River, before arriving home after visiting friends on the way.

In January 2015 I had a five-day deployment in the Adelaide Hills with other members of the NSW Rural Fire Service to assist with the extinguishing of fires at various locations and making sure that re-ignition couldn't occur.

With all our activities we don't know how I found the time to go to work, with most friends saying that 'Retirement is the busiest time of your life'.

HOW ARE WE RUNNING THE LARGEST MAP SHOP IN MELBOURNE?

MARIE MORDEN

Back in the 1990s when approaching sixty years, my husband Ian and I had thought of driving around Australia at a leisurely pace, enjoying our retirement. We already had the 4WD; we just needed a small caravan.

I thought I might run some children's drama classes or dancing classes for the older adult. But about then Ian opted to do a framing course and decided he would frame up old English county maps we had seen in the UK and sell them to people interested in family history. He wanted something hands-on after years of personnel work.

So we rented a tiny shop from a friend and he began. I kept on teaching, stopping in for awhile at the shop on the way home.

After several weeks in the shop he came home with a delighted grin on his face. He had sold his first framed map.

There was no holding him back. He found Alan Godfrey's maps of nineteenth-century England, Ireland and Scotland. These are folded maps that show how the towns were at that time and give a run-down on how they developed. They sold immediately we put them on show, and people came into the shop and asked did we have maps of how to get to Sydney (or Perth or Alice Springs or London) so we approached map wholesalers and got a small number of current maps into stock.

To make ourselves known to the family history buffs, we offered ourselves as speakers at country family history groups and were quite popular, I think because we shared the talking and often disagreed. It was fun too, meeting people all over Victoria, and even up to Queensland, and oh the country suppers! I stopped teaching about then and joined Ian in the shop. It was novel and interesting and we were rather pleased with ourselves. The bookkeeping was negligible then – a good time to start learning.

Within two years or so we realised we were outgrowing our tiny shop and started looking for a bigger one. I don't remember even discussing if we wanted to continue doing all this.

Before we found a shop I found a lump in my breast which was breast cancer. I was lucky; it had not spread. I had it removed and within weeks we moved into our new shop, from which we still operate. We had not thought this through. We knew nothing about running a shop but we found suppliers and others in the business were generous with information, and advice, particularly the Hema representative, Peter Davis, who came down every three months from Queensland, and each time was full of ideas for us to try. We expanded our stock to wall maps and bought ourselves a huge laminator for Christmas. We also began buying maps overseas to have the latest up-to-date data.

Realising our ignorance, we joined several societies and became active members.

First was the MapCircle, now the ANZ Map society, where we are 'the Commercial arm'. Most members are academics, librarians or cartographers. I became their treasurer for several years. We still attend meetings and go to the excellent conferences.

We also joined the International Map Trade Association (IMTA) and went to their meetings and conferences. This has taken us to all Australian states and on several journeys overseas.

About this time I was declared free of cancer so my daughter Alison and I set off on a tour to celebrate. I was still a bit weak, but Alison is a nurse so off we went to the IMTA Conference in Ireland. This was the first convention we went to. It was held in the Castle in Dublin. We saw the old Roman wharves under the castle, visited countless pubs to listen to Irish music with the local IMTA members and had a wonderful whiskey tasting. We also learned a lot about map sources to enlarge our stock. It was very useful to meet the producers of the maps.

Spanning the globe

We were invited to visit the Hydrographic Office in Taunton, England, the next week. There Alison and I were treated to a morning just pottering alone around the maps spread out. There was Cook's original map of the East Coast of Australia, Flinders's chart of Tasmania and of Australia, a lovely sixteenth-century Portuguese atlas hand-drawn and embellished with gold leaf. They gave us copies of several of the early unpublished maps. We spent three hours there and then were told what was on exhibition in the other countries we were visiting. So as we travelled through Europe we had the names and addresses of wonderful exhibitions along the way. As we had introductions to the leaders we were treated to talks about what we were seeing. We even saw an ancient map of the Roman Empire stretching from Britain to Sri Lanka. We visited Budapest, Prague, Vienna, and Berlin. It was wonderful. It is possible to attend these meets and just have a good time; but we learned heaps by asking questions and being interested.

Ian was really happy to see us back and listened carefully to our outpourings. He went to the next conference that was in Amsterdam and enjoyed that just as much as we had loved our trip. Since then Ian and I have managed to go together to Cesky Krumlov in the Czech Republic and later to Dresden three years ago. Each time we venture overseas we head to UK first to visit our son Bruce who lives there, and try to vary our route each time on the way home. The shop finances the trips; we only go if we have had a good year and have someone reliable to mind the shop in our absence.

One of the bonuses of running the shop is that we have been able to provide part-time employment to our teenage great-nephew and great-nieces as they did their university degrees. This has led to a close knit family. They have learned the basics of business management from us and we have had the freedom to travel in university breaks. Our own children were already into their own careers by the time we started the shop, but Richard does our excellent web page, and Bruce in the UK fixes our computers by long distance when they go wrong. I consider this twenty-first century magic! Becoming competent on the computers and the web has been a constant challenge. The support from our younger generations has been essential to our success.

Now we lead a very full life, with the shop each day, meetings for our groups, family at the weekend and occasional trips away. Alison has two beautiful small boys we visit whenever we can get to Northern NSW. Also our youngest son Robert and his partner Katherine have a two-year-old here in Melbourne. We visit most weekends and enjoy him immensely.

We still do not know the future of our business but we will enjoy it while we can. We learn something from our customers almost every day. Life is GOOD.

NOW IS THE TIME TO 'FLY'!

DI SUTTON

The sixtieth birthday party I gave myself ushered in my 'golden' years and the happiest and most fulfilling time of my life. I had reached the time of life where I wanted to celebrate my achievements and me so far. I increased the mortgage, hired a lovely hall, a band, a caterer and had the best Roaring Twenties party ever.

I was still working fulltime when at sixty-three I had an operation on my knee and needed to convalesce for a few weeks. During that time I had time to reflect on what my life was going to be in retirement, as that would be happening in a few years' time. I knew I wanted something which would help me continue my personal growth journey, to make a contribution or difference in people's lives and to earn a small income.

The answer came after about six weeks of reflection and talking with friends and confidantes – it was life coaching. This was a great fit and felt so right. Within three weeks I was enrolled in an institute in Melbourne and began six months of intensive study. Completing this was a challenge as my full-time job was very demanding, so I gave up my social life for that time. A small sacrifice for the benefits I have gained.

My business was registered when I was almost sixty-four. Helping empower people on their journey through life inspires me and gives my life meaning. I cannot adequately describe the sense of connection, joy and privilege that I experience with my clients. It is job satisfaction second to none. Another benefit is that I am evolving too and the people I continue to meet and work with enrich my life. This is the happiest time of my life; my world is continually expanding, I am more at peace with myself, I am so grateful for so much – family, grandchildren, friends, new learnings and new experiences. I am not sure what is ahead of me but have a sense it will be positive and also if challenges arise (as they do) I will be able to deal with them.

One of the largest challenges I had was learning how to establish and run a small business, after being an employee all my life. I attended seminars, had personal coaching, learned about business plans, keeping financial records, marketing, including having business cards printed and developing a website. Extensive networking has enabled me to meet potential clients and make other valuable connections. This has been an opportunity for me to make connections with, and for, other small business owners and led me to many new experiences.

I have been running my life coaching and education business for six years now, and believe that I 'walk the talk' that this can be the best time of your life. With the wisdom and experience we have gained, our fifties, sixties and seventies are a time to spread our wings and 'fly'.

I have just written a one-day seminar to help people plan for the last third of their life – to see it as a time of continual opportunity where one's world can expand. Where one can discover one's life's work, which may be different from the job one held before retirement. The workshop I have written encourages people to look at their attitudes/perceptions towards health, communication/relationships, leisure, finding meaning and purpose and caring for themselves.

Making a contribution is one of my major values and last year I voluntarily ran six workshops on communication and listening skills for unemployed people over forty at DOME (Don't Overlook Mature Expertise) and followed this up with complementary coaching. The participants and I learned a lot in this exercise and I always feel privileged to share part of a person's journey with them.

Many of my clients have been mature women, sometimes at a crossroad in their life, realising that something was stopping them being where they wanted to be. After years of caring for families or significant others, it was time for them but something was preventing them taking the next step. In the year after I retired, I took five trips to Sydney and trained in Matrix Therapies, which is a program that enables people to discover and clear what has been holding them back. In every case, there was something in their childhood that had been long repressed that needed to surface and be cleared in a non-threatening environment. One young man came to me because he could not understand what was stopping him applying for a job in Melbourne, similar to the one he had in

Adelaide, and paying much more. It took only two sessions for him to 'clear' the block and within six weeks he was happily settled in a new job in Melbourne.

As mentioned before, personally I am on a continual journey of raising self-awareness and gaining in wisdom, and apart from coaching, I make time for adventure and pleasure in my life. I know how important caring for oneself is and all that entails. For me, part of that is reading wonderful historic novels, going to deep and meaningful movies, movies of opera productions from London, Paris and New York, keeping fit, spending enjoyable time with my grandchildren and friends, and embarking on short and longer trips. I am continually meeting new people through the networking activities, especially younger people.

An attitude of youthfulness sustains and intensifies our involvement in life in ways that enable us to thrive, regardless of our chronological age. I agree with the statement that one must be very mature to exhibit youthfulness, with youthfulness being an attitude of vitality, freshness and honesty that brings colour, life and love to a person.

I have no regrets – my whole life has been a preparation for the person I am becoming now, and living life with meaning and purpose means that each day is a new possibility for giving, receiving and being grateful.

THE THIRD STAGE

DAVID SCRIMGEOUR

On my sixtieth birthday, five years ago, I had a positive feeling that I had reached a significant landmark. There was the sense that I was entering a new stage of my life, which could be thought of as the third stage, with the first being childhood and adolescence where learning was the main activity, and the second being the stage with work and bringing up children as important activities. The third stage, I hoped, would allow opportunities for activities which I still wanted to undertake with perhaps less pressure from work and family commitments. There was also the sense that the next stage was now the only opportunity for such activities – there would not be another stage after this one.

One activity I looked forward to was travel. It was not as if I had not previously travelled. In fact, I had travelled quite extensively, when I was younger as a backpacker in Asia, Europe and North and Central America, then later for study in the USA, and for work in Africa, Asia and the Pacific. However, there were other parts of the world I wanted to see, and other people to travel with. In particular, there had been increasingly frequent conversations with my three brothers, all keen travellers, suggesting that at some time we should all travel together. Two years ago, this aspiration was fulfilled.

The four of us were able to find the time, and the destination we chose was Central Asia. For three-and-a-half weeks, the four of us travelled by plane, train and hire car through Uzbekistan, Tajikistan and Kyrgyzstan, exploring the ancient cities of Kiva, Bukhara and Samarkand, the cosmopolitan cities of Tashkent and Bishkek, the stark beauty of the Pamir mountains, and the beautiful but politically troubled Fergana Valley.

Prior to the trip, we were not sure how well we would travel together as a group of four old codgers, but we all had a wonderful experience and enjoyed the time we spent together. We decided there should be further brothers' adventures, and currently we are planning a trip to Spiti, a remote Indian province high up in the Himalayan ranges, adjacent to the Tibetan border.

Travelling to Central Asia involved taking time off from work. Until recently, I have had a fulltime job, working as a public health physician with a statewide peak body for Aboriginal community-controlled health services, providing advice and support for medical and public health programs within these services. A significant part of my working life (the second life-stage) was spent working in Aboriginal health in various parts of Australia, particularly in remote areas, as a general practitioner and public health physician. I commenced the position with the statewide peak body at the age of fifty-eight, and this seemed a logical extension of my life's work. It has been satisfying, but busy.

The time has come for a change in pace with regard to paid work. I have given notice that I will soon finish working with the peak body. I will continue to work part-time, but more at the grass-roots (or perhaps, in this case, spinifex-roots) once again. Some of my most fulfilling work experiences have been spent living and working in remote communities in the beautiful Australian desert regions, and recently I have had the opportunity and privilege to return to this work. I have accepted a position as Medical Director for the primary health care service at Tjuntjuntjara, arguably the most remote community in Australia. This involves a monthly visit to the community, staying for a number of days to provide clinical and public health support to the primary health care team working there, and providing off-site support between visits (which is facilitated by the fact that electronic health information systems enable me to access health records in real time on my home computer).

Desert regions remote communities

In addition, I am an independent director with the board of the Pintupi Homelands Health Service, the community-controlled primary health care service for the remote community of Kintore, where thirty years ago I was the first doctor to work with the newly established health service. The board consists mainly of elected community people; there are also two independent directors, one providing management and governance advice, and another (me) to provide advice on primary health care and clinical governance issues. I travel to Kintore four times a year for board meetings. The board directors take their role seriously and provide very useful community input and oversight into the running of the health service, which is delivering high-quality primary health care to people living in the community. It is a privilege to be part of it.

These arrangements allow me a wonderful opportunity to have an ongoing close relationship with Aboriginal people living in close connection with their country and traditions. It also allows time for other activities, including travel, but also reflection, reading and writing, and spending time with my wife, as well as my three offspring as they complete their first life-stage, and enter the second life-stage of careers and families.

I have concerns, however, about the world into which they are launching their second life-stage. I have been dismayed to witness the odious ideology of neoliberalism become relentlessly embedded in the policies of both of the major Australian political parties the past three decades or so, leading to unacceptable economic and political inequality and insecurity, and a disregard for the significant environmental challenges confronting us. My political awakening occurred when I was a university student during the time of the Vietnam War, and my political activism has waxed and waned somewhat since then, although I have always maintained a political awareness. With a little more time on my hands, I will maintain some political activity. To paraphrase Dylan Thomas, 'I will not go gently into the good night. Old age should burn and rage at the close of day. I will rage, rage against the dying of the social democratic light'.

Wakefield Press is an independent publishing and distribution company based in Adelaide, South Australia. We love good stories and publish beautiful books. To see our full range of books, please visit our website at www.wakefieldpress.com.au where all titles are available for purchase.

Find us!

Twitter: www.twitter.com/wakefieldpress
Facebook: www.facebook.com/wakefield.press
Instagram: instagram.com/wakefieldpress

CPSIA information can be obtained
at www.ICGtesting.com
Printed in the USA
BVOW05s2333011017
5983BVAU00001B/2/P